Benjamin Franklin

Benjamin Franklin

Stephen Krensky

DK PUBLISHING

DK

LONDON, NEW YORK, MUNICH,
MELBOURNE, AND DELHI

Editor : John Searcy
Publishing Director : Beth Sutinis
Designer : Mark Johnson Davies
Art Director : Dirk Kaufman
Photo Research : Anne Burns Images
Production : Ivor Parker
DTP Designer : Kathy Farias

First American Edition, 2008

08 09 10 11 12 10 9 8 7 6 5 4 3 2 1
Published in the United States
by DK Publishing
375 Hudson Street
New York, New York 10014

DK books are available at special discounts
when purchased in bulk for sales
promotions, premiums, fund-raising,
or educational use. For details, contact:

DK Publishing Special Markets
375 Hudson Street
New York, New York 10014
SpecialSales@dk.com

A catalog record for this book is available
from the Library of Congress.

ISBN 978-0-7566-3528-2 (Paperback)
ISBN 978-0-7566-3529-9 (Hardcover)

Printed and bound in China
by South China Printing Co., Ltd.

Photography credits:
Front Cover by The Print Collector / Alamy
Back Cover by Visual Arts Library
(London) / Alamy

Discover more at
www.dk.com

Contents

chapter 1

A Boyhood in Boston

When Josiah and Abiah Franklin added another boy to their family on January 17, 1706, the event went largely unnoticed. People in Boston, Massachusetts, were used to the Franklins bringing babies into the world. Young Benjamin would be the eighth of their ten children, and the last boy. He was also the youngest son of a youngest son going back five generations, a fact that was much remarked on although it had no claims as a special omen.

At the time, Boston was a bustling town of about 7,000 people.

This 1723 view of Boston shows off its port, which was the busiest in the American colonies at this time.

Founded in 1630, ten years after the Pilgrims landed in Plymouth, it was the biggest town in the British American colonies. Most people in those colonies lived near the water, either the Atlantic Ocean or one of the major rivers—the Connecticut, the Hudson, or the Potomac farther south. Only a few miles inland from these waterways lay a vast frontier.

Benjamin Franklin was born in this house, which is no longer standing. The area is now part of Boston's financial district.

The port of Boston was busy with ships coming and going from Africa and the West Indies (now known as the Caribbean Islands). This triangle of trade was very profitable. The West Indies sent molasses to New England where it was turned into rum. The rum was then carried to Africa where it was traded for slaves. Finally, the slaves were taken to the West Indies to be traded for molasses that was sent to New England. (Few people were troubled about the trafficking of slaves in those days, although that would change over time.)

This trade supported both the shipbuilding and fishing industries, and made Boston a very prosperous town. In fact, it could even boast of having its own newspaper, the *Boston News-Letter*. Smaller cities

MOLASSES

Molasses is a thick brown syrup. It is made from the sugar cane plant, which is mashed and then boiled to release the juice inside.

This illustration of young Benjamin blowing his new whistle appeared in O.L. Holley's 1854 biography.

such as New York or Philadelphia could not say the same.

In such a bustling atmosphere, there was plenty of work for men who were skilled at working with their hands. Blacksmiths, carpenters, millers, and shoemakers all prospered at their crafts. Josiah Franklin was one of these "leather apron men" (marked by the leather aprons they wore while they worked). He was a tallow chandler, a maker of soap and candles, and he expected his sons to be tradesmen, too. Benjamin's eldest brother Samuel was already a successful blacksmith. But in such a big family, there were tragedies as well as triumphs. Two of Benjamin's brothers had drowned before reaching adulthood. One had run away to sea and was lost on a ship that never returned to port. The other died at the age of 16 months after falling into a tub of soapsuds.

Nothing so dramatic happened to Benjamin. However, he did learn a hard lesson about money early on. When he was seven, he received a half-pence coin as a holiday gift. Without delay, he went directly to a shop where toys were sold. There he met a boy who had just purchased a whistle. What sounds it made! The boy offered to give Benjamin the whistle in return for his half pence, and Benjamin was happy to oblige. He then returned home and happily shared the sound of the whistle with his family (though they were not as happy to hear the sounds as he was to make them). Only later did he learn that he had paid the boy four times what the whistle was worth. It was a painful lesson. Years later, he recalled the moment in his autobiography: When he had reviewed all the other things he might have bought with the extra money, "the Reflection gave me more Chagrin than the Whistle gave me pleasure."

The Franklins lived on Milk Street, not far from the water. (Boston was surrounded on three sides by the Charles River and the ocean, so water was never at much of a distance.) Like his friends, young Benjamin learned to swim well. But unlike them, he studied his surroundings with an unusually observant and curious eye. He even conceived of two scientific experiments in the water. Once he made oval wooden pallets to wear over his hands when he swam. He found that as he struck the water with the flat pallets, he could swim faster.

This illustration, also from Holley's biography, shows Franklin swimming with the aid of his kite.

In Franklin's time, the headmaster of Boston Latin School was Nathaniel Williams, who was also a graduate.

Another time he was flying a paper kite near the edge of a pond. It was a warm day, and while he was enjoying flying the kite, he also wished to go for a swim. In a moment of inspiration, he realized he could do both. He lay on his back in the water, holding the kite string above him. When the wind blew, the kite moved forward—and Benjamin got a free ride across the pond.

Benjamin was a natural leader, and sometimes he led his friends right into trouble. One time, for example, he came up with the idea of building a wharf over a pond. The wharf would give him and his friends somewhere dry to stand while they were fishing. To make it, the boys carried some stones that were conveniently piled nearby. They didn't worry about whether the rocks had been piled there on purpose. But they should have, since the stones were intended to be used in a house foundation. When the theft was discovered (which didn't take long since the boys had made no attempt to

WHARF

A wharf is a platform like a dock that is built along bodies of water to provide a place to stand or to go on board a boat or ship.

hide their efforts), the stones were quickly returned.

Benjamin's intelligence was clear to his parents, and at first they thought he might follow a different occupation from his brothers. Maybe he should be properly educated. He could grow up to be a preacher—the loftiest goal for a bright boy of limited means. So they sent him off to Boston Latin School, which offered the opportunity of a classical education.

Benjamin was a good student. By the end of his first year, he was at the head of his class. However, his father was having second thoughts about this school business. Education was expensive. It was a luxury that not everyone could afford. For Benjamin to become a minister would require at least ten years of schooling—six at Boston Latin School and then four more at Harvard College, across the river in Cambridge. Now, being a preacher was prestigious, but you couldn't eat prestige. And was it really such a good idea for Benjamin to spend so many years learning to read and write? What would he have to

Harvard College

Harvard College was founded in 1636, one year after Boston Latin School, so that its graduates would have somewhere to go. In Franklin's youth, there were only two other colleges in the American British colonies—Yale College in Connecticut (founded 1701) and the College of William and Mary in Virginia (founded 1693).

show for his trouble—a poor ministry with a worn frock coat and holes in his stockings?

So Josiah Franklin took Benjamin out of Boston Latin and sent him to a regular school to learn simple writing and arithmetic, skills he would need to go into business. Two years later, Josiah decided that Benjamin had learned enough to make his way in the world, and his schooling ended. It was time, his father thought, for Benjamin to start earning his keep.

But what was Benjamin to do? Why, work for his father in the candle shop, of course. Unfortunately, making candles from animal fat was smelly and boring. Some skill was involved, but it was easily learned and very repetitive. Benjamin cut wicks for the candles, filled the dipping molds, tended the shop, and went on errands. Nothing about the job required him to think or write—the two things that he loved. And the schedule was also crushing. Working more than twelve hours a day, six days a week, left little time for anything else. And for a boy who liked to read and write, this could be very frustrating.

Candles were made from different kinds of wax, some of which came from plants and others from animal fat.

Time passed slowly, but still it passed. When Benjamin was 12, he was old enough to formally become an apprentice.

In that position, he would serve a master that worked at a trade such as blacksmithing or tailoring, for perhaps seven to ten years. (The apprentice and master would agree on the exact number before the apprentice began.) During these years, Benjamin would

gradually learn the craft. After that, he could go out on his own and start a business for himself.

If Josiah had gotten his way, Benjamin would have become apprenticed to him. That was the natural order of things. Benjamin, however, was less than eager to oblige his father. In fact, he hated the idea. He was fed up with soap and candles. He could hardly imagine another decade in such drudgery. Even worse, his only reward for surviving the apprenticeship would be keeping the job for the rest of his life.

Josiah could have ordered Benjamin to follow in his footsteps, but that was a risky step to take. There was always the chance that Benjamin would refuse the order and simply run away to sea. (Indeed, Benjamin, like his ill-fated brother before him, was intrigued about the prospect of adventures aboard a ship.) Having lost one son already to the ocean deep, Josiah didn't want to lose another. Reluctantly, he agreed that Benjamin could look elsewhere to find his life's work.

2

The Young Apprentice

Josiah Franklin took Benjamin to visit a number of tradesmen. They saw joiners, bricklayers, and mechanics, among others. But not all these crafts were created equal. Some, like Josiah's, required little skill or equipment. They had less prestige, being dirtier or smellier or simply easier to do. Others, like goldsmithing, required considerable training and expensive materials. This ranked them nearer the top.

Did any of these occupations appeal to Benjamin? Not really. From top to bottom, none seemed to match his personality or capture his curiosity. Finally, it occurred to Josiah that since Benjamin had always been fond of reading, perhaps he should become a printer. And most conveniently, Benjamin's older brother James had just returned from England to open a printing shop. The Franklins had a tradition of apprenticing younger brothers to older ones, and James would need an apprentice. Benjamin was not immediately convinced—the idea of

Some of the tools on this joiner's bench were more difficult to use than others. An apprentice would spend years learning to use them properly.

Using a printing press was faster than making copies by hand, but each project still involved many hours of work.

going to sea still appealed to him. But his father persuaded him to stay.

And so, 12-year-old Benjamin Franklin signed a contract, known as papers of indenture. This was no small moment. This contract stated that from that time forward until he was 21, Benjamin agreed to serve under the care and supervision of his big brother. He would not be paid for his efforts, but James would provide him with meals, clothes, a place to sleep, and an education in the craft of printing.

Almost at once, Benjamin put his natural business sense to good use. James was responsible for Benjamin's meals at a boarding house (James didn't cook for himself), and Benjamin thought the meals provided were more than he needed. After experimenting with cooking, Benjamin made a proposal to his brother.

JOINER

A joiner is a skilled carpenter who works with wood in homes and buildings, making cabinets, and installing other wooden architectural details.

If James would pay him just half of what the boarding house charged for meals, Benjamin would take all responsibility for feeding himself. James happily agreed to this proposal. This arrangement turned out well for them both since Benjamin soon discovered he could feed himself on half of the money James gave him. The rest he pocketed to spend on other things.

As a printer's apprentice, some of Benjamin's duties had little to do with printing itself. He swept the floors, kept the fires, and

Printing presses had not changed much since their invention in the 1450s. Franklin would use this one in London.

carried messages for his master. But Benjamin paid close attention when James was working. He wanted to learn as much as he could. Each page of any printed material was made separately. Every letter of every word had to be set individually on the printer's plate—and they had to be set backward from right to left because the printing process reversed whatever was set on the plates.

After each page was printed, the letters had to be removed from the plates and put back into compartments in the proper cases so that they could be easily found again for the next job. Capital letters were kept in the upper case, while the others were kept in the lower case. (This later led to the terms *uppercase* and *lowercase* being applied to the letters themselves.) In each of these cases, the most commonly used letters—*a, e, t, s, r, n, i,* and *o*—were placed in the middle. Rarely used letters like *q, x,* and *z* were placed in the bottom left corner where they would stay out of the way until needed.

In the course of his work, Benjamin met other apprentices around town. He became especially friendly with booksellers' apprentices since booksellers often served as publishers and would hire the Franklins to do their printing. Benjamin was soon able to convince his new friends to loan him books overnight with the promise that he would return them unharmed in the morning. Sometimes, he went without sleep in order to finish a story or some collection of essays that had to go back the next day.

But Benjamin wanted to do more than learn facts from what he read. He wanted to learn style,

Pilgrim's Progress

Pilgrim's Progress, by John Bunyan, was published in 1678. It is the story of a character named Christian who travels from the City of Destruction (the earth) to the Celestial City (Heaven) while overcoming many hurdles along the way.

This picture shows Franklin trying to sell his poems to passersby—many of whom probably couldn't even read.

Franklin, enfant.

too. Even at his relatively young age, he had ambitions to become a better writer. Among his favorite books were John Bunyan's *Pilgrim's Progress* and Plutarch's *Lives of the Greeks and Romans.* He also studied newspapers and other publications, including the *Spectator,* an English newspaper. This was the work of two noted writers, Richard Addison and Joseph Steele. As Benjamin himself later wrote, " I bought it, read it over and over, and was much delighted with it. I thought the Writing excellent, and wish'd if possible to imitate it." Franklin practiced his writing by making notes about the *Spectator* articles and then rewriting them to see if he could approach the quality of the originals. Doing this taught him to express his thoughts more clearly and organize them better as well.

Benjamin also read works of poetry. Before long he was trying out his own poetic muscles. His brother encouraged him in this because original poems could be printed and sold on the street, and thus serve as an additional source of income for the shop. Benjamin's first attempt was an account of a recent tragedy, the drowning of a sea captain and his two daughters. The other was a sailor song about the infamous pirate Blackbeard.

Although both poems caused a positive stir around town, Benjamin's father was not pleased with this development. He ridiculed Benjamin's efforts. "Verse-makers were generally beggars," Josiah claimed, a practical rather than a literary view. Benjamin didn't really agree, but since he wasn't set on being a poet, there was no point in arguing. Instead he would concentrate his efforts on prose.

The most likely place to get short works of prose printed was a newspaper. And luckily for Benjamin, or so he thought, James now published one of his own, the *New-England Courant.* Several of James's friends wrote pieces for it, and Benjamin wanted to try writing some, too. But he suspected that his brother would object. James would protest that the 16-year-old Benjamin was too young,

Blackbeard

Blackbeard (1675–1718) was the nickname of pirate Edward Thatch. Brandishing swords, knives, pistols, and strands of burning rope woven into his hair, he struck fear into the hearts of the victims he overtook at sea. Blackbeard was eventually killed in a sea battle off the coast of North Carolina. He was reportedly shot and stabbed many times just to make sure he was dead.

This page from a 1722 issue of the *New-England Courant* shows how little space was wasted in filling the paper.

too inexperienced, to see his thoughts in print. It was one thing to write little verses to be sold on the street. It was quite another to express opinions on the issues of the day.

Therefore, Benjamin decided to write something secretly and submit it under another name. Not long thereafter a letter supposedly penned by a Mrs. Silence Dogood appeared under James's door. And James, suspecting nothing, was happy to make her literary acquaintance. Benjamin invented a whole background for this respectable woman. She was a "middle-aged widow," the former wife of a country minister, and a "hearty Lover of the Clergy and all good Men, and a mortal Enemy to arbitrary Government and unlimited Power." And she liked to express her opinions. Between April and October of 1722, Mrs. Dogood wrote 14 letters that were published in the *New-England Courant*.

Neither James nor the *Courant*'s readers were aware of Mrs. Dogood's real identity. And the readers never discovered it. But James did after Benjamin confessed—and he was not pleased. Benjamin was only a boy. He needed to know his place. It was not appropriate for a lowly apprentice to show up his master.

Soon, the relationship between Benjamin and his brother would grow even more complicated. Samuel Shute, the royal governor of Massachusetts appointed by the British government, did not like the *Courant*'s independent tone, and he found an excuse to throw James in jail for being critical of him. (Under the laws of the time, it was not necessary to prove James guilty of anything in court. The governor could take such actions just for being insulted.) During the three weeks James was behind bars, Benjamin was left to publish the newspaper himself.

It wasn't long before the *Courant* offended the government again. This time Shute went even further. From now on, he ordered, everything James printed would have to be approved before publication. This was a crippling order. However, it was

Young Benjamin learned quickly from his brother, perhaps too quickly to suit James and his friends.

directed only at James as the owner of the *Courant*. It was not aimed at the newspaper itself. So to get around this edict, James decided to make Benjamin the newspaper's official publisher.

But to do that, James had to dissolve the contract that bound Benjamin to him as an apprentice. (A lowly apprentice would not be allowed to publish a newspaper on his own.) Publicly, Benjamin was now free to be his own master. Privately, however, the two brothers created a new secret contract to cover the remainder of Benjamin's apprenticeship.

As an apprentice, Benjamin had little time to call his own after fulfilling all his chores and duties.

This arrangement worked well enough for several months, at least on the surface. But Benjamin was becoming more and more frustrated. He was tired of doing the ordinary chores of an apprentice, setting up type, selling publications on the street—when he did not benefit more directly from the work. And he was eager to do more writing as well.

Benjamin became angrier and angrier. If his brother would not give him more responsibility, then he would leave. An apprentice, of course, would not have that option, but technically Benjamin wasn't an apprentice. As far as the world was concerned, Benjamin could do as he pleased. James could stop him by revealing the existence of the secret contract, but Benjamin figured that was unlikely. If James did that, he would be admitting that his transfer of the newspaper to Benjamin had been a fraud. It wasn't hard to imagine what the governor would think of that.

But even if James could not stop Benjamin from leaving, he could still speak to the other printers in town and make sure they didn't hire his brother. Faced with unemployment or the prospect of going into a whole new line of work, Benjamin decided to leave Boston. But where should he go? Within the colonies, his choices were limited. He sold some of his books to raise the price of a ticket and then boarded a ship. Three days later, as he later wrote in his autobiography, "a Boy of but 17, without the least Recommendation to or Knowledge of any Person in the Place, and with very little Money in my Pocket," landed in New York.

This map of New York from 1755 shows the concentrated development at the southern end of Manhattan Island.

chapter **3**

Journeyman Printer

New York in 1723 was a much smaller town than Boston. Founded by Dutch settlers in 1624 as New Amsterdam, its name had been changed to New York after the British conquered the town in 1664. Now, with a population of just over 7,000, the people lived in a jumble of streets at the southern tip of Manhattan Island. To the north were some

Philadelphia was a common starting point for pioneers wishing to head west toward the Ohio Valley.

farms and a few rough paths.

Upon his arrival, Benjamin went to see William Bradford, a well-known

VUE DE PHILADELPHIE

Philadelphia

Philadelphie

printer. Bradford was polite to the former apprentice, but he had no need for an extra hand. Still, he had a suggestion: Was Franklin willing to go to Philadelphia? Bradford's son Andrew had his own shop there. Perhaps he had an opening.

Unwilling to return home, Benjamin moved on. Philadelphia was growing fast as the gateway to the southern colonies. It was the biggest city in

William Penn planned to spend more time in Pennsylvania, but financial issues kept him busy in England.

Pennsylvania, a colony given to Admiral William Penn in the late 1600s to pay off a large debt from the British crown. The admiral's son, also called William Penn, visited the land in 1682 and soon laid out the first streets for the city.

Penn was a Quaker, a member of a religious group that firmly believed in education and the advancement of science. The Quakers were also open-minded about sharing space with people who did not share their views. So the atmosphere in Philadelphia was freer than in Boston, where local inhabitants were not so tolerant of outsiders. (Over time, Franklin himself developed a straightforward approach to religion. He believed in God and the idea of doing good works, but he was tolerant of the various ways people could observe such things.)

When Benjamin first got to Philadelphia, he went to see Andrew Bradford at once. Unfortunately, the younger Bradford had no jobs to offer, either. However, he sent Benjamin along

RUE
BENJAMIN
FRANKLIN
(1706 - 1790.)
PHYSICIEN ET HOMME D'ÉTAT
AMÉRICAIN

Quakers and Puritans

In the Boston that Franklin had left behind, Puritan leaders did not encourage the exchange of ideas at odds with their own. Their goals were noble enough, in pursuit of a harmonious existence with God, but their attitudes could be harsh for those who didn't share their point of view. The peace-loving Quakers of Philadelphia created an atmosphere of religious freedom and were more tolerant of people simply enjoying themselves.

to another printer, Samuel Keimer, and here Benjamin's luck changed. Keimer put him to work at once. And before long Benjamin came to a surprising conclusion. He realized that he was already a better printer than either Keimer or Bradford. "These two printers," he wrote later, "I found poorly Qualified for the Business. Bradford had not been bred to it, & was very illiterate; and Keimer tho' something of a Scholar, was a mere Compositor, knowing nothing of Presswork." Neither of these established printers had an artistic eye or a feeling for words. This conclusion encouraged Benjamin since he was firmly convinced that he possessed such skills himself.

At first, Benjamin kept his whereabouts a secret from his family. But one of his brothers-in-law, Robert Holmes, was a sea captain whose ship sailed back and forth between Boston and Delaware. He happened to hear that Benjamin was living in Philadelphia, and he wrote Benjamin a letter trying to convince him to return home.

JOURNEYMAN

A journeyman is a member of a trade who has finished his apprenticeship, but works for another person rather than owning his own shop.

Benjamin wrote back, refusing the suggestion. But Holmes was not ready to give up yet. He showed the letter to Sir William Keith, the governor of Pennsylvania. He hoped the governor would insist that Benjamin return home (although the governor had no actual power to make Benjamin go).

Upon arriving in Philadelphia, Franklin walked the streets carrying one large roll under each arm while he ate a third.

Keith's reaction, however, was not what Holmes expected. Sir William had a low opinion of the printers in Philadelphia. He was eager for a new one to set up shop, somebody more talented than the others. Perhaps young Franklin was such a man. If so, he should be persuaded to stay.

The governor then took it upon himself to search out the young journeyman. When he arrived at Keimer's shop, Keimer naturally assumed that the governor had come to see him. Sir William explained otherwise, leaving Keimer both surprised and a little embarrassed. Benjamin was surprised, too, but that didn't mean he couldn't enjoy the fact that Keimer "star'd like a Pig poison'd" at the news.

Sir William Keith eventually had to flee Pennsylvania for England in order to avoid the many people he owed money.

In the course of his business, Franklin exchanged notes such as this one in return for books or other goods.

The governor took Benjamin to a local tavern for a talk. There he encouraged Benjamin to start his own printing shop. More specifically, he promised support in the form of government printing jobs. This seemed like a tremendous opportunity. Benjamin had been in Philadelphia only a short time and already the governor himself was requesting his services. The advantage was not entirely on his side, though. It would be handy for Sir William to have a printer who would owe his livelihood to him—a printer always ready and willing to publish the governor's views.

But setting up as a printer cost money—and Benjamin had no money of his own. Sir William suggested that Benjamin convince his father to supply the necessary funds. The governor would send along a letter expressing the promise of future support.

So with a new business arrangement to propose, Benjamin returned home to Boston. His father and family (except perhaps James) were glad to see him. But Josiah had reservations about the new business. Even with a governor's support, Josiah thought Benjamin was too young and inexperienced for such a responsibility. Maybe in three years, when he was 21, things might be different.

Disappointed, Benjamin returned to Philadelphia empty-handed. But the governor was not discouraged. He told Benjamin to go to England to buy the printer's equipment he needed. Sir William offered to supply the necessary funds himself. Later, when Benjamin's business was established, he could repay the loan.

At the time only one ship sailed from Philadelphia to London each year. So Benjamin had to wait a couple of months for its departure. In the meantime, he continued to work for Keimer. Aside from that, he also started spending more time with his landlord's daughter, Deborah Read. He had first seen her upon his arrival in Philadelphia, when all he had in his pocket were a couple of bakery rolls. "I had great respect and affection for her," he wrote later, "and had some reason to believe she had the same for me." Benjamin was thinking of marriage, but Mrs. Read thought it would be better for Debby to wait until Benjamin returned from England.

When Franklin boarded the ship for London, he expected to find letters from the governor waiting for him. These letters would authorize him to get money from Keith's accounts at London banks. But after the ship

Deborah Read caught Franklin's eye the first time he saw her. This portrait from the late 1750s shows her formal side.

sailed, he found that there were no letters. Sir William Keith, for all his fine talk, was a famously unreliable fellow, and a poor one at that. Another passenger, Thomas Denham, confirmed the bad news. Denham "told me there was not the least Probability that he had written any Letters for me, that no one who knew him had the smallest Dependance on him, and he laughed at the Notion of the Governor's giving me a Letter of Credit, having as he said no Credit to give."

Under the circumstances, the trip was not a happy one. Nor was it quick. The voyage across the Atlantic took almost two months. And it was not luxurious sailing. There was little to eat except heavily salted food and hard biscuits. Seasickness was common on the small boat, which made slow headway through the cresting waves and strong winds.

Franklin arrived in England with no money, either to live on or to buy a ticket home. But with

Ships that crossed the Atlantic at this time were relatively small, with cramped quarters for the passengers.

his printing skills, he soon found work at a local print shop. From the beginning, several things set Benjamin apart from his coworkers. For starters, he was younger than most. He also ate no meat and drank no beer (habits he had taken up to save money during his apprenticeship). Avoiding both, he felt, was better for

Food Preservation

In Franklin's time, there was no way to keep food fresh on ocean voyages. It had to be protected in some way so it would remain edible for as long as possible. One popular preservative was salt, which was used in great quantities, especially on meat. Travelers soon tired of the limited diet, but with nowhere to go, they had to get used to it.

his health—and there was no question that it was better for his wallet. Beer, in particular, kept his fellow printers poor and drunk, a combination he was determined to avoid. After all, a drunken printer would forever remain poor, and a poor printer would never have enough to drink.

Despite his youth, Benjamin was bursting with confidence. He met some scholars and other important men through the printing business and hoped to meet more. One thing he didn't do while in London was write many letters home. His relationship with Debby was particularly hurt by this. Over the course of many months he only wrote her once, and it was not an encouraging letter. He had no idea when he might return home and took no pains to hide this fact from her.

Truth be told, it would not have taken much for Benjamin to stay in England indefinitely. He was making

> *"I resolve to speak ill of no man whatever, not even in a matter of truth..."*
>
> —Benjamin Franklin, in his 1726 notes

friends, saving money, and enjoying the activities that a city like London had to offer. Compared to London, Philadelphia was a frontier outpost. And then Thomas Denham, his fellow passenger on the voyage out, searched him out to make a proposition. Denham wanted to open a store back in Philadelphia, and he wanted Franklin to be his clerk. If everything worked out, there was the promise of further financial gains in the future. Also, as part of the arrangement, Denham would pay for Franklin's passage home.

By the 1700s, London had become the financial center of the world. Following the great fire of 1666, the city was growing in every direction.

LEICESTER SQUARE, ABOUT 1750.

The offer was good one, and spurred by a twinge of homesickness, Franklin accepted. They sailed on July 22, 1726. Again, the voyage was a long one, leaving Franklin plenty of time alone with his thoughts. But he spent this time productively, composing a philosophy about how he should lead his life. His list of resolutions reflected his upright and conservative way of thinking:

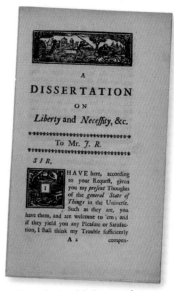

1. It is necessary for me to be extremely frugal for some time, until I have paid off what I owe.

Never losing his interest in writing, Franklin wrote and published this pamphlet during his time in London.

2. To endeavor to speak truth in every instance, to give nobody expectations that are not likely to be answered, but aim at sincerity in every word and action . . .

3. To apply myself industriously to whatever business I take in hand, and not to divert my mind from my business by any foolish project of growing suddenly rich . . .

4. I resolve to speak ill of no man whatever, not even in a matter of truth . . .

He wrote later that he formulated this plan to guide him from that point on. He might stray from the plan occasionally, but it was more than just empty words. When Benjamin Franklin made a plan, he meant it.

chapter 4

Getting Down to Business

Benjamin Franklin thought that his days as a printer
were over. He now planned to become a merchant, and
he hoped in time to be a very successful one. In October
1726, when he and Denham arrived back in Philadelphia,
they opened the store together as planned.

Benjamin took naturally to his business work. He was
good with numbers and careful with his accounts. But
despite these abilities, he never got the chance to see if the
store would succeed. Only three months later, Denham fell ill
and died—bringing an abrupt end

Franklin oversaw all aspects of
his printing business, making
sure both the writing and the
production met his standards.

to his business, and leaving Benjamin without a job.

Other young men might have bemoaned their bad luck, but Benjamin was not like other young men. Shrugging off his setback (and a lengthy sickness of his own), he went back to work for Samuel Keimer. With the experience he had gained in London, he was no longer an inexperienced journeyman. Keimer put him in charge, and Benjamin quickly had the shop in good running order. Before long, however, Keimer tried to cut his wages in an attempt to save money. Benjamin didn't take kindly to that. He was still an impatient young man, and if Keimer did not recognize his good fortune in having Benjamin work for him, then Benjamin would try his luck elsewhere.

With one of his fellow workers, Hugh Meredith, Benjamin set up his own printing shop. It was a partnership between his intelligence and the money Meredith's father

Early English-language Newspapers

The first real newspaper in English was the *London Gazette*, first published in 1666. In the American colonies, the first newspaper was the *Boston News-Letter*, which first appeared in 1704. Only a few pages long, it was published weekly, which was often enough to keep up with the news. Other items were also included to fill out the space, along with advertisements (there was only one in the first issue). Daily newspapers did not appear until the 1780s, when events moved fast enough and readership grew large enough to support more frequent publications. Larger populations also meant a wider variety of coverage and a greater need to stay current.

In his first years in business, Franklin could not afford many employees so he had to make his own printing deliveries.

supplied to get the business going. And before long, Benjamin used that intelligence to come up with a very promising plan.

From his experience in the industry, Benjamin had already learned that a printer should not rely solely on work from others to prosper. What if days or weeks went by and no customers walked through the door? It was prudent to create some original printing, like the newspaper his brother had published in Boston.

And thus, the idea was born: Why not start a newspaper of his own? The task suited his talents well. A newspaper was not just the news of the day. It included stories and bits of advice—just the kind of thing Benjamin was good at concocting.

At the time, the only existing newspaper in Philadelphia was the *American Weekly Mercury* published by Andrew Bradford. Benjamin considered it "a paltry thing." But before he took any further steps, his plans came to Keimer's attention. And the next thing Benjamin knew, Keimer started a newspaper himself. He called it the *Universal Instructor in all Arts and Sciences: and Pennsylvania Gazette.*

Unfortunately, the newspaper was as labored and dull as its title suggested.

Franklin, of course, was angry to see Keimer steal his idea. In revenge, he started writing for Bradford's paper. He hoped that his contributions would stimulate sales and harm the fledgling *Gazette*. And in this he succeeded. Within nine months the *Gazette* was floundering. Keimer then decided he wanted to sell it, hoping to earn a little something for his trouble. Franklin, smiling at least to himself, was more than willing to buy it at a bargain price.

As a new publisher, Benjamin did not publish the Gazette to cause trouble or stir up controversy. His goal was to make a profit. And if his writing abilities made his paper more lively and interesting than anyone else's, then the profits would surely come.

In fact, Benjamin's business grew in all areas. Soon he was able to buy out his partner, Hugh Meredith. His energy was not entirely focused on his career, though. His personal attentions had turned

The *Pennsylvania Gazette* looked much like other papers of the time. What set it apart was Franklin's skill as a writer.

back to Deborah Read. Benjamin's relationship with Debby had faded during his trip to England. Eventually, Debby had cast her interest elsewhere and married another man. However, this husband had now left her and disappeared. There were rumors that he was dead or had gone back to London (where he may have actually had another wife). In any case, he seemed gone for good.

Francis Folger Franklin's death from smallpox was not unusual. The disease claimed thousands of lives in the colonies.

None of this potential for scandal seemed to trouble Benjamin. He courted Debby successfully, and clearly she was happy to receive his attentions. Under the custom of the time, Debby and Benjamin could not marry because of her uncertain married status. But it was acceptable for her to join Benjamin in a common law marriage—and that's what she did. They moved in together in September 1, 1730. Benjamin was happy with their relationship. Debby, he wrote, "assisted me cheerfully in my business, folding and stitching pamphlets, tending shop, purchasing old linen rags for papermakers etc. etc."

Only a few months later, Benjamin became a

COMMON LAW MARRIAGE

A common law marriage is one that becomes legal after a couple has spent a certain time living together and presenting themselves as married.

father. It is not clear, however, whether the mother of his son was Debby or another woman. Whatever the truth, little William was raised as their

son. Two years later, in 1732, Franklin's second child, Francis Folger, was born. Although Francis died from smallpox at the age of four, Sally Franklin, born in 1743, would prove to be a more lasting addition to the family.

Meanwhile, as a good businessman, Benjamin was always on the lookout for new ventures. He opened a shop next to his printing business that sold stationery supplies and other items related to printing. Later, he also sold coffee, tea, cakes of soap from the family business in Boston, and Rhode Island cheese. (Benjamin also saw the value in not having to rely on others for his own supplies— so he made a point of buying paper mills,

Franklin's ambition and practicality helped establish him as one of Philadelphia's leading businessmen.

Poor Richard, 1733.

AN

Almanack

For the Year of Chrift

1733,

Being the Firft after LEAP YEAR:

And makes fince the Creation Years

By the Account of the Eaftern *Greeks* 7241
By the Latin Church, when ☉ ent. ϒ 6932
By the Computation of *W. W.* 5742
By the Roman Chronology 5683
By the Jewish Rabbies 5494

Wherein is contained

The Lunations, Eclipfes, Judgment of the Weather, Spring Tides, Planets Motions & mutual Afpects, Sun and Moon's Rifing and Setting, Length of Days, Time of High Water, Fairs, Courts, and obfervable Days.

Fitted to the Latitude of Forty Degrees, and a Meridian of Five Hours Weft from *London,* but may without fenfible Error, ferve all the adjacent Places, even from *Newfoundland* to *South-Carolina.*

By *RICHARD SAUNDERS,* Philom.

PHILADELPHIA:

Printed and fold by B. *FRANKLIN,* at the New Printing-Office near the Market.

Franklin was inspired by some of the writing of British author Jonathan Swift when creating the character of Poor Richard.

and a lampblack factory to keep himself supplied with ink.)

Franklin's printing business relied on two main sources. His ordinary customers hired him to print advertising handbills, miscellaneous forms, or other one-time needs. And then there were clients (including the city and colonial governments), whose jobs were bigger and likely to be repeated. One early commission that helped Benjamin's reputation was printing paper money for the colony of New Jersey. This was a complicated task that took three months to complete. It benefited Franklin in two ways: He was paid well, and the job also brought him into contact with influential people who had sophisticated printing needs of their own.

The *Gazette* was not the only publication Franklin backed to increase his business. In 1732, he first published *Poor Richard's Almanack.* The almanac (the *k* was eventually taken out of the title) was a mixture of historical facts, weather predictions, poems, jokes, and other bits of information from daily life. Franklin created the character of Richard Saunders to introduce the annual almanac, and Poor Richard proved to be so popular that Franklin kept him around for the next 25 years. The folksy character introduced himself this way:

Courteous Reader: I might in this place attempt to gain thy favor by declaring that I write almanacs with no other view than that of the public good, but in this I should not be sincere; and men are nowadays too wise to be deceived by pretenses . . . The plain truth of the matter is, I am excessive poor, and my wife, good woman, is, I tell her, excessive proud; she cannot bear, she says, to sit spinning in her shift of tow, while I do

Lively pictures such as this one were important to spurring almanac sales.

nothing but gaze at the stars; and has threatened more than once to burn all my books and rattling traps (as she calls my instruments) if I do not make some profitable use of them for the good of my family.

Poor Richard was a big success, eventually selling about 10,000 copies a year, a big number in a country of less than two million people. Many found Poor Richard's advice both wise and funny, which was a powerful combination. "If you would not be forgotten as soon as you are dead and rotten," said Poor Richard, "either write things worth reading, or do things worth the writing."

Freemasons

In 1731, Franklin joined the freemasons, an ancient and secretive organization dedicated to fellowship and good works. Among its members were many of Philadelphia's most prosperous merchants, and Franklin was always alert to the ways that good social contacts could improve his business.

While Franklin's business was growing, he was also interested in stretching his mind. In 1733, he helped start a club formally called the Junto (the Latin word for meeting). Informally, it was known as the Leather Apron Club because its 12 members worked with their hands for a living. They gathered together to discuss various philosophical, historical, literary, and scientific issues, challenging one another in friendly debates. The Junto proved to be very popular and soon other people were asking to join. But Franklin liked the club's small size and suggested instead that others form new clubs along similar lines.

Still very much a reader, Franklin proposed to the Junto that they put their books together where they could be shared. This small common library never really got started, but a larger subscription library, where members paid a fee to belong and take out books, was more successful. The first order for books was placed in 1732, and the library grew so quickly that it soon required its own building.

As Benjamin's reputation grew, he attracted more and more

In later years, Franklin would still give the mail and last-minute instructions to post riders about to depart.

An organized fire company had the skill and equipment necessary to successfully combat large fires.

valuable contracts. He was already the official printer for Pennsylvania, and he soon added Delaware and New Jersey as customers. In 1737, he became the deputy postmaster of Philadelphia. In this position, he used his organizational skills to plan better postal routes and more frequent mail-delivery schedules. The job did not pay particularly well, but it gave him some distinct advantages. He knew about news from other places before anyone else did and he could distribute his newspaper for free along the postal routes instead of paying for the privilege.

As a practical man of the city, Franklin was always looking for ways to improve the general quality of life. Fire was a big risk to any group of buildings in close quarters, and Franklin proposed creating Philadelphia's first volunteer fire department in 1736. Crime was also a problem, and Franklin saw here too the advantages of creating a local force—supported by taxes. These constables could concern themselves with public safety on a street-by-street level (something the king's soldiers would never bother with, being too busy protecting the borders).

Franklin also looked to the advantages of paving streets and hiring people to collect trash.

As much as he liked to make money, though, Franklin had his limits. "In order to secure my Credit and Character as a tradesman," he observed, "I took care not only to be in Reality Industrious & frugal, but to avoid all Appearances of the Contrary."

One day he was asked to publish something that he found rude and objectionable. However, the assignment would turn a nice profit for him. So the question arose in his mind: Should he take the job or not? To help him decide, he spent the night sleeping on the floor and then ate only bread and water for dinner and breakfast. "Finding that I can live in this manner, I have formed a determination never to prostitute my press to the purposes of corruption, and abuse of this kind, for the sake of gaining a more comfortable subsistence." And so he turned the job down.

Volunteer firefighters of the period carried buckets of water like this one to help refill the engine pumper.

As shown by this incident, Franklin was keenly interested in developing the proper moral habits—and, as it turned out, he was not prepared to leave this development to chance. Expanding on the ideas he had first written on the ship from London to Philadelphia, he compiled a list of virtues that he hoped would anchor his behavior

Franklin often had to work long hours to ensure the success of his business and writing ventures.

at all times. Among them were:

Temperance: Eat not to dullness, drink not to elevation.

Silence: Speak not but what may benefit others or yourself; avoid trifling conversation.

Order: Let all your things have their place; let each part of your business have its time.

Resolution: Resolve to perform what you ought; perform without fail what you resolve.

Frugality: Make no expense but to do good to others or yourself; i.e., waste nothing.

Industry: Lose no time; be always employed in something useful; cut off all unnecessary actions.

Sincerity: Use no harmful deceit; think innocently and justly; and if you speak, speak accordingly.

Justice: Wrong none by doing injuries, or omitting the benefits that are your duty.

"I took care not only to be in Reality Industrious & frugal, but to avoid all Appearances of the Contrary."

—Benjamin Franklin, in his autobiography

Moderation: Avoid extremes; forbear resenting injuries so much as you think they deserve.

Cleanliness: Tolerate no uncleanliness in body, clothes or habitation.

Tranquility: Be not disturbed at trifles, or by accidents common or unavoidable.

One of the criticisms aimed at Franklin was that the warmth of his business skills was not matched by the warmth of his heart. But those voicing this opinion often opposed either his political aims or his business views. He may have been tough on his competitors, but he was honest and fair. And if it turned out that he was more talented than his peers, he could hardly be blamed for that. However, it may also be true that Franklin was as much concerned with the appearance of being good as he was with actually being good. Whether or not Franklin always practiced what he preached, he did a pretty good job most of the time. And his determination in this regard clearly helped him succeed in other areas of his life.

In 1741, Franklin tried his hand at publishing a magazine, but he stopped after a few issues due to low sales.

THE GENERAL MAGAZINE, AND Hiſtorical Chronicle, For all the Britiſh Plantations in America. [To be Continued Monthly.]

JANUARY, 1741.

ICH DIEN

VOL. I.

PHILADELPHIA: Printed and Sold by B. FRANKLIN.

chapter **5**

Ideas and Inventions

Benjamin Franklin lived at an interesting crossroads in scientific history. On the one hand, men such as Sir Isaac Newton (whose lifespan overlapped Franklin's) had revolutionized our view of the physical world with his insights into gravity and the laws of motion. On the other hand, people were still being convicted of witchcraft and burned at the stake.

Almost 150 years earlier, Sir Francis Bacon (who coined the phrase "Knowledge is power") had introduced the scientific method as a way of investigating natural phenomena. This involved performing experiments to impartially evaluate the theories scientists had about the world. Those who agreed with Bacon did not believe that nature should be frightening. The physical world was meant to be understood. Of course, it might contain mysteries, but these were mysteries that could be solved.

Sir Francis Bacon conducted many experiments during his life. In his last one, he stuffed a chicken with snow to study the preservation of meat.

Franklin clearly shared this view. And more than that, he wanted others to share it as well. However, for people to hold scientific opinions, they would have to be educated first. So in 1743 Franklin proposed creating an academy in Philadelphia, a school that would take students beyond a basic education. However, the time was not right for this initiative. Philadelphia was busy worrying about attacks from the French and Spanish, who, as was often the case, were at war with the English.

These struggles reflected the conflicting claims of European powers in the New

Isaac Newton

Sir Isaac Newton (1642–1727) revolutionized our scientific understanding of the universe. His *Principia Mathematica*, published in 1687, lay the foundation for classical physics. The mathematics needed to support his ideas didn't exist beforehand. Newton had to invent them himself in order to complete his work.

World that had begun in the days of Columbus. And by the 1700s, with no more land available to claim, these countries often went to war with one another, hoping victories on the battlefield would further enlarge their territories.

The dangers from the current conflict—known as King George's War—eventually prompted the people of

Philadelphia to raise a militia for its defense. (Although Quakers did not believe in armed conflict, the city now contained enough non-Quakers to make this feasible.) As a major backer of the militia, Franklin was asked to be in charge. But he declined the position, citing his lack of experience in military matters. It was one of the few honors he ever refused.

Unable for the moment to promote science in education, Franklin pressed forward in other areas. In 1744, he founded the American Philosophical Society to foster the exchange of scientific views. Unlike the Junto, the Society was not meant to be composed of Philadelphians alone. Franklin wanted it to include members from all 13 American colonies.

Library Hall is one of several buildings owned by the modern-day American Philosophical Society.

Clearly, Franklin encouraged and liked the idea of sharing information with other people. The most dramatic example of this attitude was his refusal to patent any of his inventions. "As we enjoy great advantages from the inventions of others," he wrote, "we should be glad of an opportunity to serve others by any invention of ours; and this we should do freely and generously."

University of Pennsylvania

Franklin's academy was finally launched in 1749. Unlike the existing colleges in the American colonies—Harvard, Yale, and William and Mary—which focused on a classical education for training the clergy, Franklin wanted the school to have a broader educational purpose. Within 30 years of its founding, the school had grown into the University of Pennsylvania.

One of Franklin's strengths was his ability to see larger questions in the details of everyday life. One time, for example, he discovered some ants that had gotten into an open pot of molasses. He carefully removed them all, except for one. He then suspended the pot from some string, which he attached to the ceiling, directing the extra string down an adjoining wall. Eventually, the one remaining ant followed the string up, over and down to the floor. Franklin waited. About half an hour later, the pot was again filled with ants. Franklin wondered how the one ant had told so many others about the food waiting for them if they followed him back over the string.

Franklin was especially intrigued by ideas that could be tested by physical means. When he heard that a speaker was

The Pennsylvania Fire-Place, or Franklin Stove, was popular not only in the American colonies but in Europe as well.

addressing 30,000 people in the open air, he questioned the truth of this. To satisfy himself, he measured the maximum distance from which he thought a speaker could be heard in an outside area. Using this distance as the radius of a circle, he determined how big a circular space people could stand in and still hear a speaker in the middle. Then he determined how many people could stand in that circle. It turned out to be more than 30,000, meaning the original report was not necessarily an exaggeration.

As much as he delighted in such observations, Franklin tended to concentrate his efforts on more practical matters. And few things were more practical than keeping warm. Even at that early date, American colonists were using up forests at a noticeable rate. A more efficient use of wood was desirable, both to maintain the fuel supply and to make houses more comfortable.

Franklin had noticed that existing stoves had two major problems. The first was that they were smoky, making it uncomfortable to sit near them. Second, they were not efficient about radiating heat.

Franklin's solution was to invent a stove that fit into the fireplace. (Existing fireplaces were handy for cooking, but not very good at heating up rooms. Franklin's stove did both.) In his design, the stove was enclosed on three sides, so the heat was directed properly out into the room. But this was not his only innovation. The flue for his stove was also important. It doubled back on itself, giving the heat more time to radiate into the room before it shot up the chimney. These new stoves went on sale in 1744 and were immediately popular anywhere in the colonies where winter made its presence felt.

Many of Franklin's experiments had very definite beginnings and endings. But his investigation of electricity went on for decades. He first became interested in electricity during a visit to Boston in 1743. He saw a demonstration by Dr. Archibald Spencer from Scotland in which sparks were made to fly from a child's hands and feet.

At that time it was generally thought that there were two kinds of electricity because of the

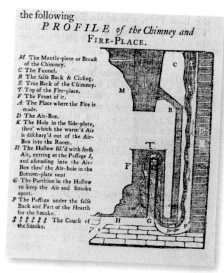

Franklin was happy to make diagrams of his stove available so that anyone interested could understand how it worked.

way it presented itself in different situations. Franklin, however, believed that there was only one kind of electricity, which "was not created by friction, but collected, being an Element diffused among, and attracted by other Matter, particularly Water and Metals." Moreover, he stated that electricity must be composed of tiny particles that could move easily through metals.

One important piece of equipment used in electrical experiments was a Leyden jar. This was a glass jar with a stoppered top, some water

Franklin used this vacuum pump to remove air from a closed container, allowing him to study electricity in the absence of air.

at the bottom, and a metal rod reaching down from the stopper to the water. When the bottle was charged with electricity, it would give a shock to anyone who touched it. Franklin wondered how the a Leyden jar could collect and store such a shock. After several experiments in which he removed parts of the bottle, he determined that it was the glass that held the charge.

Franklin's investigations into electricity reflected the same care and thoroughness that he brought to everything else.

And his creativity extended even to the language of his work. As he went along, he coined words such as *conductor, battery, charge,* and *discharge* that were soon adopted for general use in electrical research.

Franklin had time for all these activities because his businesses were doing so well. His financial security was so assured that he officially retired as a printer in 1748. At that time, he formed a partnership with his foreman, David Hall. The terms stated that Franklin was to be paid 500 pounds a year (about half of the royal governor's salary and more than nine times what a teacher of the period earned) for 18 years. After that, Hall would own the business alone.

Of course, all of these advances did not come without some costs. Some of Franklin's fellow Philadelphians were jealous of his success. Others disapproved of his sharp business practices, especially people he had outsmarted in the past. To silence such criticism, the 40-year-old Franklin could simply have retired to a life of leisure. In fact, he was just getting started.

If one Leyden jar could hold a charge, Franklin reasoned that a group of jars (which he called a battery) could hold much more.

chapter **6**

Inspired Impulses

Nobody was more practical than Benjamin Franklin. He ate and dressed sensibly. He was careful about his health. When it came to business, he analyzed situations and made decisions based on facts and figures. If he started a magazine and sales were disappointing, he stopped publication. If an item in his shop didn't sell, he stopped stocking it.

But when it came to science, this practicality was blended with a passionate curiosity. Franklin was intensely curious about the world, both the big and the little things. True, some of his investigations led to profitable ends, but that was not his only motivation. Scientific questions were worth answering for their own sake.

Much of his attention had already focused on electricity. In 1751, a comprehensive account of Franklin's electrical experiments was published in London. The 86-page pamphlet was simply called *Experiments*

This distinguished painting, made by Robert Feke around 1746, is the earliest known portrait of Benjamin Franklin.

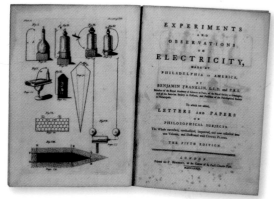

The title page of Franklin's pamphlet included several diagrams of devices used in his electrical experiments.

and Observations on Electricity Made at Philadelphia in America by Mr. Benjamin Franklin. The pamphlet did not make headlines with the general public, but the scientists who read it were properly impressed.

One of Franklin's experiments concerned the question of whether clouds that produced lightning contained electricity. He described a way to confirm this by drawing out electrical sparks from a tower during a storm. But before he could try the experiment himself, a French scientist, using Franklin's suggestions, beat him to it. However, Franklin still got much of the credit for coming up with the idea. Within a year, his work had made him famous in Europe.

Meanwhile, in June 1752, Franklin was doing a further investigation of thunderstorms. Any simple observation of such storms showed that lightning accompanied them. But was the lightning separate and distinct from the rest of the storm, or part of it? And was the lightning made of electricity? Or was it some other kind of energy such as light or heat?

Franklin determined that he could start to find the answers to these questions simply by using a kite. His son William,

This 19th-century print by Currier and Ives captures the public's idea of how Franklin conducted his kite experiment.

then in his early twenties, assisted him. First, Franklin made a kite with two sticks and a large silk handkerchief. He then added a piece of wire that extended about a foot beyond the bottom of the kite. To hold the kite he added a long piece of string. At the end of it, he tied a key with a silk ribbon.

When a storm approached, Franklin directed William to run across a field to get the kite into the sky. Once the kite was aloft, William gave the string to his father. At first Franklin saw nothing to indicate the presence of electricity. But then he noticed some stray threads of the string standing straight up. Franklin had seen this effect before when electricity was present, and so he touched the key at the end of the string.

He felt the spark at once.

Franklin believed that this spark had come from the lightning itself, demonstrating that lightning was indeed a form of electricity (and not, as many people thought, some kind of supernatural punishment from the heavens). Having established this, he wanted to put that information to good use. His idea was simple. Instead of waiting for lightning to strike a building—and start a fire or cause some other damage—why not redirect the lightning so it could do no harm? To do this, Franklin envisioned a long piece of metal that would stick up higher than the highest point of a building. A wire attached to this metal rod would run down the building and into the ground. Since lightning tends to strike the highest point in an area, it would strike the rod instead of the building. Then the electricity would be led down the wire and into the ground, where it wouldn't cause any trouble.

Franklin described the lightning rod in his almanac of 1753. Some people, believing that lightning was a punishment from God, feared that God

This 19th century engraving depicts the first installation of a lightning rod on a house in Philadelphia in 1760.

would not be pleased if people tried to protect themselves from his anger. Others reconciled themselves to the idea of the lightning rod through the belief that God helps those who help themselves. Either way, Franklin made no defense of his invention. He never defended his scientific views. As he wrote, "I leave them to take their chance in the world. If they are right, truth and experience will support them; if wrong, they ought to be refuted and rejected."

This umbrella, designed by Franklin, incorporated a lightning rod to protect the user during storms.

Franklin's investigations did not always lead to inventions, though. Many years later, for example, having crossed the Atlantic several times, he had noticed that the journey was shorter when traveling from America to England than when going the other way. The reason, he soon learned from sea captains, was the existence of the Gulf Stream. This ocean current helps carry ships from west to east, but when ships travel in the other direction, they must fight the current, and so are slowed down. Despite sailors' awareness of the Gulf Stream, it had so far not been noted on navigational charts. Franklin had the current marked out for him, and he published new charts showing the Gulf Stream to help sailors with future crossings.

As a postmaster and almanac publisher, Franklin also took special notice of the growing American population. In his role as deputy postmaster general, he had already made the service between cities more frequent. For example, he increased the service between Philadelphia and New York from once to three times a week in the summer. In 1750 he published an essay about the population trend. He stated that in 100 years, the population in America would exceed that of England. As a businessman, he saw great significance in this. Currently, colonists bought all their manufactured goods from England,

After learning about the Gulf Stream, Franklin created this map of the current to aid sailors in their navigation.

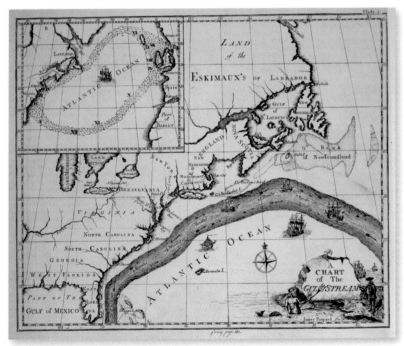

but someday the demand would be too great for that practice to continue (despite the best efforts of British manufacturers). At some point, the colonies would need to develop a manufacturing base of their own.

However, Franklin was not as open-minded as he might have been about the question of who should be part of that growing population. He was particularly troubled by the German immigrants who made a point of keeping to themselves, observing their own customs and language in a kind of cocoon separated from the outside world. In his view, people who came to the colonies should make every effort to adopt the colonial ways. In fact, he did not welcome anything that smacked of foreign customs or habits.

Another phenomenon that bothered Franklin—and other Pennsylvanians—a great deal was

This painting depicts the 1683 treaty between William Penn and the local Indians. The agreement was unusually fair for the time.

the worsening situation between themselves and the Penn family. Pennsylvania was different than the other colonies because one family, the Penns, owned so much of it. They lived in England, and for the most part they had little personal interest in Pennsylvania. All that mattered to them was squeezing as much money as possible from their property.

They didn't care about the people who lived there, and they didn't care about any problems these people might be having.

As the problems facing the Pennsylvania colonists grew larger, the Penns' attitude became a larger issue as well. High on the colonists' list of concerns was colonial security. Ongoing dangers from both French forces and their Indian allies were a problem up and down the frontier. At a 1754 conference in Albany, New York, Franklin and other colonial representatives met with members of the Iroquois Confederation (a group of Indian tribes) to discuss their complaints and to create a treaty to keep peace with the Iroquois.

Franklin's first impression of American Indians in the 1740s had not been a positive one. Certainly, they didn't share his values and outlook on life. But this opinion changed

This woodcut shows a Mohawk Village in central New York as it would have looked around 1760.

over time. And as he eventually noted, "Almost every war between the Indians and whites has been occasioned by some injustice of the latter toward the former."

As the colonists met with the Indians, Franklin's superiors in London were only concerned with getting a treaty to cover the current fighting—but Franklin was hoping for more. He was aiming for a permanent understanding between the Iroquois and the American colonies.

The Plan of Union that the representatives devised was a compromise between many different people and interests. It proposed an organization governing all the colonies. This organization would have a president appointed by the King of England. There would also be a council with representatives from each colony.

Franklin and his fellow negotiators were more enthusiastic about their plan than anyone else was. All the colonies soundly rejected it. None of them were ready to give up any individual power to a centralized colonial body. As for the British, they were not interested in creating any independent government in America—even one still loyal to England. They liked the system the way it was: they told the colonies what to do, and the colonies did what they were told. And since the English and French continued their war in the colonies for the next seven years, nobody else was thinking too hard about anything beyond the fighting itself.

Franklin was upset to see his plan defeated, but he was even more troubled by the British government's attitude toward the colonies. The government did not appear to look upon the colonists as loyal subjects deserving its respect. Instead, it seemed to consider the colonies as a treasure chest to be dipped into whenever it wanted. This attitude, Franklin concluded, was not just. At some point, things would have to change.

Meanwhile, the jostling between the Penns and the Pennsylvania colonists was only getting worse. Franklin spoke out about it and about the rights and liberties of the people. Finally, the Pennsylvania Assembly (which represented the colonists) decided to send Franklin to London as its agent. He was glad to have a chance to visit England again. The hope was that more direct negotiations would be productive for achieving progress with the Penn family. Whether this hope was realistic, though, remained to be seen.

Franklin published this 1754 cartoon in the *Pennsylvania Gazette* to underscore the need for the colonies to band together.

chapter 7

Going Abroad

The Benjamin Franklin who returned to London in 1757 was a very different person from the journeyman printer who had gone there more than 30 years before. Then he had been an unknown and penniless traveler. Now he was both a prosperous man of business and a respected scientist. Benjamin the successful printer might have gone unnoticed in London, but Franklin the scientist and inventor was too well-known a figure to ignore.

Franklin had left Philadelphia thinking the trip would be

B. Franklin of Philadelphia
L.L.D. F.R.S.

a relatively short one. He took his son William with him to act as his secretary. William was in his late twenties now, with a taste for adventure. At 16, he had tried to run away to sea (as his father had once thought of doing). His father talked him out

James McArdell's 1761 portrait depicts Franklin as a scholar and a scientist. Lightning can be seen in the background.

This painting depicts a 1759 sea battle between England and France, part of the two nations' ongoing war.

of that, but later arranged for him to accompany a military expedition to Canada. Now William was finally taking his first trip overseas.

Franklin hoped the rest of his family would come along as well. But Debby was afraid of the sea and would not cross it. In addition, she simply felt comfortable in the familiar ways of Philadelphia. So she and their 14-year-old daughter Sally stayed behind.

Actually, Debby was not wrong to be wary of such trips. The voyage to England was marked by efforts to evade any French ships they met along the way, since England and France were at war. The captain worked so hard to achieve this that he almost ran the ship aground off the English coast.

But Franklin and William arrived safely at last. They settled into some very pleasant living quarters, taking rooms with a widow, Mrs. Margaret Stevenson, and her daughter Mary. The arrangement almost seemed like having another family, and Franklin quickly felt right at home.

Franklin found London to be an exciting place, bursting with energy and ideas. But the city did have its drawbacks. Countless chimneys billowed forth smoke and soot in the name of industrial progress. In a letter to Debby, Franklin complained that it wasn't possible to get a real breath of fresh air without riding out far into the countryside.

As the representative of the Pennsylvania Assembly, Franklin's first duty was to convince the British government to start taxing the Penns' land holdings. As we've seen, Pennsylvania's situation was unusual among the colonies because of the way it had been founded. The Penns owned the original land and they continued to

Sir Thomas Lombe's 18th century silk mill in the town of Derby spews forth smoke in the name of progress.

control it and receive rent from those who lived and worked there. They didn't pay taxes on their holdings, which hadn't been so bad when there wasn't much reason for the local government to charge anyone for services. But as Pennsylvania's population had grown, the need for services had grown, too. And the fact that everyone else had to pay for them made the Penns pretty unpopular.

William Franklin owed much of his success to his father, but came to disagree with him on the rights of the colonies.

The Penns, however, understood better than Franklin how little influence he held. He might have represented the interests of Pennsylvania, but here in England Pennsylvania was a very faraway and unimportant place. And the Penns didn't mind being unpopular in Pennsylvania—as long as they got paid. The Penns also made it clear that they did not believe that colonists had the rights of British citizens. The fact that Pennsylvania had changed so much in the 80 years since its founding made no difference to them.

And there was more. The Penns were aristocrats, well established in the halls of power. Franklin was the son of a tradesman who made soap and candles. He might have applied some polish to his humble origins, but, in the Penns' eyes, that hardly made him worth recognizing. In truth, the Penns had no wish to reach a happy compromise, or even an unhappy one. But they were content to prolong the discussion

Benjamin Franklin lived in this house on Craven Street during the years he spent in London, representing the colonies.

for as long as possible to make it appear that they were honestly negotiating.

In scientific circles at least, Franklin was a name of importance. His published work on electricity and other matters prompted many social invitations. And while the business of lobbying was not always fun, it often took place in pleasant settings. Much of the work was done over grand dinners topped with fine wines. Franklin always maintained that, while he was a plain person himself, with modest habits, this job required him "to live in a fashion and expense, suitable to the publick character I sustain'd." This was not exactly a hardship, though, and by all accounts Franklin enjoyed every minute of it.

Of course, not all of Franklin's time was spent attending meetings and knocking on doors. He and William took many trips outside of London. On one they explored the ancestral home of the Franklins, seeing the place where Benjamin's father and grandfather had been born. They also toured the Midlands and Scotland for three months in 1759. On this trip, the University of St. Andrews gave Franklin an honorary degree. The degree stipulated that Franklin should now be referred to as a doctor, and from this point on he was often called "Dr. Franklin."

Still, Franklin's work as a colonial agent was frustrating and slow. One of the upsetting things he was learning was that Parliament didn't feel obligated to consult colonial legislatures before making laws that affected them. Apparently, Parliament did what it pleased where the colonies were concerned—and, to make matters worse, colonists were not allowed to vote for members of Parliament. But Franklin saw how shortsighted this attitude was. Surely the British government didn't think that it could treat these people as second-class citizens forever. Could they really be so blind?

Through all the political ups and downs, Franklin finally finished his official work in London in 1760. Although he had enjoyed only limited success as an advocate for the Pennsylvania Assembly, he had at least gotten the British government to agree that the Penn lands were taxable. He did not, however, rush home at once. Instead, he stayed on for

This engraving shows a 1760 session of the House of Commons, one of the two houses of Parliament.

another two years. One reason was that he was simply enjoying himself. For example, he attended the coronation of the new king, George III, in October 1761. George was 22 and enjoyed a fine reputation. Franklin had every reason to think he would do well on the throne.

That same year, Franklin put his creativity to use again with his design for a new musical instrument, the glass armonica.

King George III

King George III (1738–1820) will always be linked to the American Revolution, although his reign extended for 39 years after the war was over. He ruled at a time when the king still had significant power over the government of England. After 1801, he was increasingly incapacitated by an illness that caused blindness and senility.

He was inspired after seeing a musician play music by touching wine glasses filled with different amounts of water. Franklin's armonica was a series of glass hemispheres ranging in size from three to nine inches (8 to 23 cm). The glasses were held on a spindle that could be rotated by a foot treadle. The sounds were made by wiping slightly wet fingers against the glasses. Combinations of notes could be produced by wiping more than one glass at a time. Admittedly, the armonica was never going to be featured in a parade, but

The armonica made interesting and haunting musical sounds, but it remained more of a novelty than a popular instrument.

it was another worthy accomplishment for a man who'd had more than his share already.

Another reason Franklin remained in England was to help William further his career. Some British government officials no doubt saw a chance to gain Franklin's loyalty by giving his son an important position. This was the likely reason William Franklin, though lacking any real administrative experience, was named royal governor of New Jersey in 1762.

Finally, after five years abroad, it was time to return home. As he crossed the Atlantic again in the fall of 1762, Franklin continued to spend his time in scientific study. He measured the water temperature, marked the strength of the currents, and made lists of the birds and fish he encountered. The voyage took a long time because, as before, the ship was trying to avoid French vessels (England and France were still at war).

Philadelphia looked good to Franklin after such a long time away. He was glad to see Debby and Sally again, and to meet up with his old friends. But he was also sorry to leave England. Franklin had predicted that the reign of the new king would be "happy and truly glorious." It wasn't long, however, before Franklin's optimism was put to the test.

8

Back to England

The latest war between England and France finally ended in 1763. The British had emerged as the victors, leaving the French on the losing side, and the terms of the peace treaty removed France as a power in the eastern part of North America.

This was good news for the British colonists—or at least it should have been. But peace for the colonies came at a steep price. One of the treaty provisions prohibited colonists from heading west into the frontier of Ohio. The British government didn't want to pay to protect them there. It was easier to keep them away.

This decision did not sit well with the increasingly independent Americans. By the 1760s, many of the colonists were not as closely tied to England as their parents and grandparents had been. More and more of them had been born in America and had

Mason Chamberlain's 1762 portrait of Franklin reflects the work he was doing in England on behalf of the colonies.

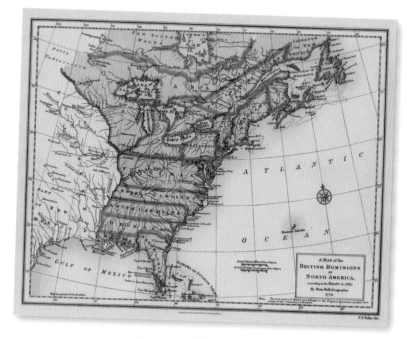

This map shows the extent of the British colonies in 1763. Some stretched from the Atlantic to the Mississippi.

never even visited England. What business did a government 3,000 miles (4,800 km) away have telling them where they could and couldn't go, without even asking their opinion?

Clearly, the colonies and the British government were at very different points in their thinking. With the threat of war with France removed once and for all, the colonists were eager to develop their land with no outside interference. The British government, on the other hand, was looking to repay itself for the cost of the war. Since the colonists would benefit the most from the peace, the British naturally thought the colonists should pay dearly for their good fortune.

Amid all this controversy, Franklin returned to England in 1764. As before, his job was to represent the interests of Pennsylvania, especially with regard to raising money for the colony's support. And soon he would become the agent for Georgia, New Jersey, and Massachusetts as well.

Franklin created this cartoon to express opposition to the Stamp Act, showing that its burden was too much to bear.

Franklin wanted the British government to understand that the American colonists would not follow its directives blindly. But the government ignored his warnings. It began by creating new taxes on sugar, coffee, and imported wines. Soon the British were taxing all kinds of contracts, from marriage licenses to land titles. Paper goods such as newspapers and magazines were taxed as well. Under the controversial Stamp Act, if an item was not stamped appropriately by a government agent, it could not be used or bought by the colonists.

The colonists were not happy about this. Even if the taxes were just, it didn't seem right that they had no say in how they were created. The whole situation was clearly unfair. The colonists called it "taxation without representation," and they didn't like it one bit.

Franklin thought these taxes might be reasonable at least in principle and still hoped the spirit of compromise would win out. But being in England, he missed out on the sense of outrage and anger that was steadily building back home. At one point, even his own Philadelphia house was threatened with violence from mobs who thought he was favoring the British too much. Luckily, other citizens managed to maintain order.

Under the Stamp Act of 1765, stamps like these had to be applied to a wide variety of products in the colonies.

When Franklin finally realized how earnest the colonial opposition was, he jumped in to support it. Most importantly, he spoke in Parliament in January 1766, championing the American point of view. Over several hours he answered dozens of questions in a calm and reasonable manner. Even those who opposed his views were impressed with the way he defended them.

Tensions lessened some when the Stamp Act was repealed a few months later. But this repeal did not signal a fundamental change in Parliament's thinking. It still reserved the right to tax the colonies whenever it wanted and for however much it saw fit. The colonies could protest, but that didn't necessarily mean Parliament would listen.

Franklin hoped that he could convince the government to let the colonies run themselves while still being part of the British Empire. He spent a lot of time meeting other scientists and diplomats, many of whom had a special interest in colonial life. Franklin foresaw that America would become a very powerful part of the British Empire, "able to shake off any shackle that may be imposed on her ..." It would be wise, he thought, for England to give her room to grow.

The problem was, nobody in England was used to thinking this way. Empires were usually built by conquering people from other places.

This 1774 painting dramatizes the fate of any tax collector unlucky enough to fall into the hands of angry colonists.

The conquered people had no rights because that was considered the price of being conquered. But the vast majority of citizens in the American colonies hadn't been conquered at all. They had come to America of their own free will. They were looking for a better life, and they were willing to work hard for it. They were also willing to fight for that life if they thought anyone—including their own government—was threatening it.

By 1768, the British government was almost entirely lined up against the colonial point of view. The British insisted that their power over the colonies was absolute. Their ministers had too much pride to step back and see the situation as something unique in their history, and therefore deserving of a unique approach.

The latest tax imposed upon the colonies came through the Townshend Acts, which placed new taxes on tea,

Sally Franklin

In 1767, Franklin's 24-year-old daughter, Sally, married Richard Bache, an English merchant who had moved to the colonies. The first of their seven children was named Benjamin Franklin Bache. Sally was always close to her father, despite not seeing him for the many years he lived in England. She would eventually care for him in his old age.

16ᵉ Arrᵗ
RUE
BENJAMIN
FRANKLIN
(1706 - 1790)
PHYSICIEN ET HOMME D'ÉTAT
AMÉRICAIN

CUSTOMHOUSE

A customhouse was a building where government officials processed paperwork relating to goods that were entering or leaving the American colonies.

paper, glass, and paint. The dissatisfaction over these events was no longer just a rumbling. It was reaching a steady roar. Some groups, such as Boston's Sons of Liberty, were already floating the idea of independence. Others still remained loyal to England.

But tempers were growing short. On March 5, 1770, a crowd gathered around some British soldiers who were guarding the Boston customhouse. Pelted with snowballs, the guards panicked and fired into the crowd. Five Americans were killed and several others were wounded. From the colonial standpoint, the Boston Massacre, as it came to be called, was the latest and most tragic example of the British disregard for American lives.

Amid all the political turmoil, Franklin maintained his scientific curiosity. He reported the story of a bottle of wine that had been sent to him from Virginia. When the first glass was poured out, three

Paul Revere's 1770 engraving depicts the Boston Massacre as an entirely unprovoked attack by the British.

flies were discovered in the wine. Franklin put the flies on a safe perch to see what would happen when they dried out. Two of the flies actually revived and flew off, unaware that they had traveled to a new country. Franklin commented that he wished he could be preserved in a similar fashion and revived at a later date to see how the world had changed in the meantime.

Franklin is thoughtfully engaged in his work in this picture, derived from a 1767 portrait by David Martin.

Perhaps with a sense of his posterity in mind, Franklin started working on his autobiography in 1771. He began the book as a letter to William and covered the first 25 years of his life before stopping. He wrote the first part in less than two weeks. One of his goals was clearly to show that a practical nature and hard work could lead to great success, regardless of the circumstances of one's birth. Franklin made no attempt to be complete in every detail. He wrote about the things he was interested in writing about, which was mostly his philosophy and his work.

In 1770, anger over the Townshend Acts led to their taxes being repealed on everything but tea. Nonetheless, ill feelings on both sides of the Atlantic continued to grow. As the most prominent colonist living in London, Franklin found himself the focus of angry attention, and as a public backer of the colonial cause, he came under increasing attack.

THE DESTRUCTION OF TEA AT BOSTON HARBOR.

The enthusiastic bystanders in this lithograph of the Boston Tea Party emphasize the act's popularity with colonists.

Things only got worse after the Boston Tea Party of 1773. That incident started when three ships arrived in Boston filled with tea, the one item still being taxed after the repeal of the Townshend Acts. The Sons of Liberty wanted the ships to leave. But the governor, Thomas Hutchinson, wasn't interested in their opinion. So on the night of December 16th, a group of colonists dressed as Mohawk Indians boarded the ships and threw 95,000 pounds (43,000 kg) of tea into the harbor.

The British responded by closing the port of Boston. This harsh measure crippled the city, affecting protesters and loyalists alike. Franklin still hoped that the differences between the colonies and England could be resolved peacefully. But he could also see that things were heading toward some sort of climax, peaceful or not. The current level of tension could not last forever.

When Franklin next went to speak before government officials, he was soundly criticized in a long and personal attack. The fact that Franklin was only the legal representative of the colonies no longer mattered. He was here in the room, while the colonies and all its rabblerousers were thousands of miles away. They were out of reach for the moment. Franklin was not.

Fortunately, Franklin stayed calm under fire. He did not say a word. He could see that words could no longer heal the breech between the colonies and the crown. The next day he lost his job as deputy postmaster general. The message was clear: If he was not a clear supporter of the crown, then the crown was not his supporter, either.

Christian Schussele's 1859 painting dramatizes Franklin's appearance before the Lords in Council in 1774.

At this point, Franklin thought about going home, but he received word from America that he should stay a little longer. There might be things he needed to do.

Meanwhile, in September 1774, the First Continental Congress met in Philadelphia. This was a gathering of representatives from all 13 American colonies. By the meeting's end, the delegates had decided to cut off all trade with England. If the King and the British government did not respect their liberties, then they in turn would not consider themselves bound by British laws. They also demanded the repeal of every act aimed at them since 1763.

When Franklin spoke with his friend, the scientist Joseph Priestly, he was still steering a middle course in the dispute. There was no question that he thought the colonies had legitimate complaints. But he believed that these complaints could be reasonably resolved. The first step, however, was for the British government to admit that the colonists had the right to make complaints. Yet to those in power in England, this was no small request.

Amid all this political turmoil, Franklin received sad news from home. On December

This painting shows members of the First Continental Congress outside what was later called Independence Hall.

19, 1774, his wife Debby had died. She had been sick for several years, having partially lost her memory in 1768. The news saddened Franklin deeply. He cared for his wife, both emotionally and practically, although he seemed to have no trouble with their long separations. It's true that she made this situation worse by her unwillingness to travel, but the fact remains that Franklin never seemed in a hurry to go home. Still, although he could certainly survive without her companionship, it couldn't have been easy to learn of Debby's death.

Joseph Priestly

Joseph Priestly (1733–1804) was an English scientist best known as one of the codiscoverers of oxygen (along with Antoine Lavoisier of France). However, he also believed in ideas about combustion that were later proved to be mistaken. A respected philosopher and educator, Priestly spent the last 12 years of his life living in the United States.

Franklin finally left England in the late winter of 1775. No doubt he had overstayed his welcome, but he still expected to return someday. He actually told his English friends that he might come back in a few months. Of course, before that could happen, the disagreement between the colonies and England would have to be settled. Franklin believed that was possible. But by this time, not many people agreed with him.

16° Ar¹

RUE
BENJAMIN
FRANKLIN
(1706 - 1790)
PHYSICIEN ET HOMME D'ÉTAT
AMÉRICAIN

chapter 9

Fighting a War

Franklin arrived home from England on May 5, 1775. While the six-week voyage had been uneventful, life in the colonies could not say the same. Much had gone on during his time at sea—and none of it seemed likely to help keep the peace.

On the night of April 18, General Gage, the British commander in Boston, had sent troops out to capture some ammunition and other colonial military supplies located in Concord, a little over 20 miles (32 km) away. But riders on horseback—the most famous of whom was the silversmith Paul Revere—had warned the residents of the countryside of their coming. The British had met with resistance, first from a few dozen minutemen in

This 19th-century illustration shows the minutemen holding off the British troops at the bridge at Concord.

Lexington. When the two groups met, a shot was fired (from which side no one knows). A few seconds later, more shots were exchanged. Eight minutemen were killed and ten more wounded. Shouldering their rifles, the British then marched on to Concord. There they met a much larger force, one they were unable to defeat. Forced to retreat, they returned to Boston without the desired munitions and also without numerous comrades who had been killed along the way.

Unlike the earlier Boston Massacre, which had been viewed as a tragic but isolated incident, the news from Lexington and Concord was considered much more significant. The Second Continental Congress was preparing to meet in Philadelphia to discuss the new events taking place, and the first session began five days after Franklin got home.

Paul Revere

Paul Revere (1734–1818) was a man of many talents—a silversmith, a copper engraver, a businessman, and a political activist. He remains most famous as one of the riders sent out to warn the countryside that the British had left Boston and were heading for Concord. Revere himself never reached Concord, but was captured in Lexington and later released.

MINUTEMEN

Minutemen were farmers and tradesmen who made up a volunteer militia. They pledged to be ready to assemble on a minute's notice.

This lithograph shows George Washington being appointed the commander in chief of the continental army.

At the age of 69, Benjamin Franklin was the group's senior statesman.

He was not the richest delegate. Nor was he the tallest, the shortest, or the best looking. But he was the most famous.

George Washington—already an accomplished military hero and a prominent voice in the resistance—was soon appointed commander in chief of the colonial army. He now hurried to Boston to oversee the colonial troops that were surrounding the city, penning the British soldiers inside.

Franklin had hoped that violence and war could be avoided if reasonable men could be brought together on both sides. But the British, it seemed, had no reasonable men in power. And so he reluctantly accepted the necessity of war. Not that everyone was taking the colonial view. Many, including

Franklin's son William, remained loyal to England. Eventually, father and son grew so far apart in their views that they stopped communicating for several years.

Franklin's current sentiments were neatly summarized in a letter he wrote to an old friend and member of the British Parliament, William Strahan. The letter was never sent, but was widely reprinted.

> Mr. Strahan: You are a member of Parliament, and one of the majority which has doomed my country to destruction. You have begun to burn our towns and murder our people. Look upon your hands! They are stained with the blood of your relations! You and I were long friends. You are now my enemy, and I am
>
> Yours,
> B. Franklin

The Second Continental Congress met primarily at the Pennsylvania State House (now called Independence Hall).

The American forces started this war at a distinct disadvantage. They had little manufacturing capabilities, no real navy, and few soldiers trained to fight traditional battles (most of their experience was against Indians on the frontier).

And the Continental Congress faced internal hurdles as well. Other

John Trumbull's painting of the June 1775 Battle of Bunker Hill spotlights the death of colonial General Joseph Warren.

than the fact that the British were treating them badly, the delegates did not agree on much. Southern colonies had different priorities from northern colonies. Larger colonies with frontiers to the west worried about things that were of no concern to smaller colonies on the coast. It was critically important that the colonies act as one, but how that "one" should act was a matter of considerable debate.

Franklin served on many committees of the Continental Congress. Most prominent among them were the Committee of Safety and the Committee for Secret Correspondence (which communicated with potential allies around the world). In one of his roles, Franklin visited with General Washington in Cambridge, Massachusetts, to discuss army matters. There were many details to be worked out regarding the equipping of the army and the rules of engagement that specified what to do with captured soldiers or property, among other things.

The summer of 1775 saw more fighting on many fronts. The British were forced to evacuate Boston, but they made up for this with victories elsewhere. The more lives that were lost and property that was destroyed, the faster the chances of an early peace faded. In August, King George III formally declared the rebellion to be official.

On the colonial side, the rebellion had felt official for some time. Americans had been moved to independence not only by British injustice, but also by philosophical ideas. Most prominent among them was a 47-page pamphlet called *Common Sense* written by Thomas Paine. He wanted to see the colonies break away from England and create a representative democracy. Published in January 1776, *Common Sense* sold over 120,000 copies in only a few months.

Common Sense put into words what many of the colonists were already feeling, but not so clearly thinking.

Paine's text was simple and to the point. His words encouraged ordinary people to take up the cause of

Thomas Paine

Thomas Paine (1737–1809) was born and grew up in England. He lived there until 1774 when he moved to America. Although his writings helped inspire the colonists in the revolt, he played no part in the development of the United States once the war was over. His written work, however, was also an inspiration to the French Revolution of 1789.

independence—and continued to inspire them as the conflict progressed. In a later essay, he wrote: "These are the times that try men's souls. The summer soldier and the sunshine patriot will, in this crisis, shrink from the service of their country; but he that stands it *now*, deserves the love and thanks of men and women."

As the Second Continental Congress continued to meet, it evolved into a long-term governing body, which would last for the duration of the war (and was often referred to simply as "Congress"). Franklin often reminded the delegates of his Plan of Union and the importance of sticking together. But even acting with a unified front, the colonies lacked the resources of their English enemies. They needed allies, and they needed them fast.

In March 1776, Franklin and three others made a trip to British Canada to try to get the Canadians to join their cause.

It was a difficult journey, including a 36-hour crossing of 26-mile (42 km) Lake George north of Albany, New York. They reached Montreal at the end of April. Franklin felt poorly, suffering from swollen legs and boils. But even if he had been in excellent health, there would still have been little he could do. The Canadians were not interested in rebellion. And even if Franklin had been up to changing their minds, the arrival of thousands of British soldiers in Quebec cut the visit short.

Another possible source of aid was France. But the French had conflicting views of the emerging conflict. On the one hand, they were eager to find ways to weaken the British Empire, especially in light of their own monumental defeat in 1763. On the other, they were still a monarchy, and the idea of commoners successfully bucking a king's authority was not a comforting thought. Through their representatives, they told the Americans that they would take no official steps until the colonies had declared their independence.

This reaction was not completely unexpected. In fact, while Franklin had been in Canada, another committee had formed, one that included him without his knowledge. This committee was given the task of writing a declaration of American independence, a document that

Benjamin Franklin designed this silver dollar, which was issued as one of the first non-British American coins in 1776.

This 1909 painting shows Franklin, Adams, and Jefferson working on the Declaration of Independence.

would proclaim to the world the Americans' intention to be free.

That June, a committee of five—Benjamin Franklin, Thomas Jefferson, John Adams, Robert Livingston, and Roger Sherman—was set up to write the document. The main work was assigned to the 33-year-old Jefferson of Virginia.

This was not work done lightly. The participants were talking treason. And treason, if they were captured, was punishable by death. The text was mostly Jefferson's work, but Franklin made a few revisions to an early draft. It was he, for example, who suggested the notable phrase, "We hold these truths to be self-evident . . ."

On July 4, 1776, 56 delegates from the 13 American colonies gathered in Philadelphia to formally declare their independence from Great Britain. They believed the decision to secede, to break away from England, was the right one. And they had made their feelings and ideas clear in their Declaration of Independence.

> *"We must all hang together, or most assuredly we will all hang separately."*
>
> —Benjamin Franklin, at the signing of the Declaration of Independence

Almost a month later, on August 2, the delegates prepared to sign the final document. As the president of the Continental Congress, John Hancock of Massachusetts signed his name first. "We must all hang together," he commented, recognizing the moment's historical importance. But Benjamin Franklin, underscoring the risk they were taking, added a line of his own: "We must all hang together," he reportedly said, "or most assuredly we will all hang separately."

A month later, Franklin led a final delegation to the British representative, Lord Howe, in New York. Their goal was to avoid a continuation of the war. (Franklin had met Lord Howe two years earlier in England, which gave them a head start on the negotiations to come.)

The meeting with Lord Howe was friendly enough, but he was only empowered to talk about surrenders and pardons

This mural at the Benjamin Franklin Institute of Technology depicts Franklin taking his turn signing the Declaration.

for treasonous behavior. None of the issues that had led to war were up for discussion. He was hoping that these revolutionaries would simply come to their senses, admit their mistakes, and agree to end the rebellion. Further unpleasantness could be avoided if they would only return things to how they had been before.

From the British side, this offer seemed generous. What chance did these colonials have against the most powerful country in the world? And here they were being given a chance to avoid punishment and penalty—what more could they want?

Quite a bit, actually. The promise of a pardon in no way addressed the colonial grievances. Franklin and the others were in full control of their senses when they insisted that Britain must recognize that things had changed, and move on from there. But Lord Howe could not even begin to share this viewpoint. With the two sides so far apart, there was little more to do but politely say good-bye.

Up to this point, some British supporters thought that Franklin had

This 19th century painting illustrates the unsuccessful attempt at a peace conference with Lord Howe.

As shown by this 1776 political cartoon, many saw Franklin as engaging in a precarious balancing act with his loyalties.

been pretending to be moderate while secretly advocating the colonial cause. But this was not true. He was moderate at first, and truly wished the conflict to be avoided altogether, or at least to end quickly. But once those options were no longer available, he showed his practical side. If there had to be a revolution, then he would throw himself into the fray with all the energy and experience that he could muster.

Not that he wasn't hobbled a bit. At 70, Franklin felt old. He knew how important this moment was, but while that understanding strengthened his resolve, it didn't make him feel any younger. Still, when asked to go to France, he did not refuse. He agreed to join Silas Deane and Arthur Lee (the American representatives already working in Paris), hoping to convince the French to support the American cause.

On October 26, 1776, he sailed for France aboard a small sloop. For company he took his two grandsons, 16-year-old Temple (William's son) and 7-year-old Benjamin Franklin Bache (Sally's son). The boys probably enjoyed every minute of the exciting trip. Franklin, feeling queasy from every swell of the ocean waves, was just glad when it was over.

97

chapter 10

The Toast of Paris

Franklin arrived in France safely, but not in the best of health. He had told one friend that he felt like a remnant of cloth that Congress could use in whatever way seemed productive, but which was clearly no longer of the best quality. He was frail and often hindered by attacks of gout, a disease that inflamed his joints and made walking painful. Franklin was well aware that too much rich food and drink made his gout worse. Unfortunately, he was not good at resisting the temptations he met at every meal.

The weather in December was hardly welcoming, and it took almost three weeks to reach Paris from the coast. Still, the enthusiastic greetings Franklin received along the way lifted his spirits. He was well known in France as a scientist, particularly

Franklin's fur hat was meant to emphasize his image as an unpretentious American who spoke and acted plainly.

This painting shows Franklin as the center of attention during a visit to the court of French King Louis XVI.

as the inventor of the lightning rod. For diplomatic purposes, he might have preferred a quiet arrival in Paris, so that he could begin his work without the British knowing of his presence. But it was too late for secrecy, so he contented himself with enjoying the festivities.

Famous scientist or not, Franklin presented himself to the French as the rustic homespun American. He dressed humbly in plain clothes and wore a fur hat instead of a powdered wig. But Franklin's clothes were more than a simple reflection of his modesty. His job was partly to play a role. Any man who so clearly appeared to be without pretensions must obviously represent a worthy cause—or so Franklin hoped. His appearance was calculated to gain favor with the French and perhaps more support for the American colonies as well.

Despite his personal appearance, Franklin knew how to live in a grand style. After a short time residing in a Paris hotel, he

Franklin was so popular in France that the famous sculptor Jean-Antoine Houdon had him sit for a sculpture.

settled in on an estate in the nearby village of Passy. Although he kept Temple with him, he soon sent young Benny Bache to school in Switzerland. Franklin's host at Passy was a French merchant who hoped to turn a profit should the French end up aiding the Americans' efforts. Toward that end, he fully intended to see that Franklin was comfortable. And if comfort meant nine servants, the use of carriages and coaches, and access to the best wines and rum, then Franklin was certainly in the right place.

Franklin was a popular dinner guest, partly because of his accomplishments, but also because of the way he dealt with people. The other American representatives, Deane and Lee, were not so skilled. "The wit of conversation," Franklin wrote, "consists more in finding it in others, than showing a great deal yourself." And for a man who did not cut an imposing physical figure, he became friends with many women in France. Among them was Anne-Louise Brillon de Joux, who was 40 years younger than Franklin and married to a member of the French government. Another friend was the wealthy widow Madame Helvetius who was close to his own age. Franklin even asked her to marry him at one point. Although she turned him down, they continued to be close friends.

The French, both men and women, liked Franklin more universally than they supported the American cause. At first, the French government was cautious. It wished to avoid provoking the British into going to war with France yet again. They also didn't want to openly support what might quickly become the losing side. However, the French were ready to secretly make some money available, and they set up companies to supply weapons and other goods to the Continental army.

The American representatives, of course, were looking for more than financial support. If the French recognized the colonists as a legitimate independent government, other nations of the world might follow. The problem was that the American efforts in 1775 and 1776 were not encouraging. One defeat seemed to follow another, and any prospects for an eventual victory seemed dim.

Early in 1777, however, encouraging news arrived. General Washington and his forces were supposed to be on the run in northeastern

Houdon's 1778–79 bust is probably one of the most accurate images of Franklin from his later life.

Emanuel Leutze's 1851 painting of Washington crossing the Delaware captures the bold spirit of the surprise attack.

Pennsylvania. But in an unexpected move, Washington had crossed the Delaware River into New Jersey on Christmas Eve. Early on Christmas morning, his troops had surprised a large British force of Hessian soldiers from Germany. An army of colonial farmers was supposed to be no match for the 900 Hessians camped in Trenton. Yet the Americans had captured them just the same.

Across the Atlantic, Washington's first decisive victory encouraged the American representatives in their work. In addition to the ongoing quest for support, Franklin had rules of wartime conduct that he hoped Congress would implement. He was very particular, for example, about protecting the rights of neutral people and countries during wartime. Farmers and fishermen should also be respected as food providers, regardless of which side they provided for. Furthermore, he thought that enemy surgeons should never be detained as prisoners. Instead, they should be released so that they could continue their work of helping humanity. As for the countries behind the fighting, they too should be held to account. "Justice is as strictly due between neighbor nations as between neighbor citizens," he wrote. "A highwayman is as much a robber when he plunders in a gang as when single; and a nation that makes an unjust war is only a great gang."

Franklin's fame continued to make it difficult for him to accomplish much in secret. And spies were everywhere. Franklin didn't worry about them, though. His guiding principle was "to be concerned in no affairs that I should blush to have made public . . ." This claim, however, was only true up to a point. One trick Franklin employed was to print fake newspapers, supposedly from the colonies, with exaggerated reports of the atrocities British soldiers were committing during the war. He carefully chose type styles used in the colonies and included fake advertisements and notices to make the newspapers seem real. The fake papers were then taken to England and distributed. Many ordinary British citizens were horrified to read of their soldiers behaving so disgracefully, and their horror stirred up opposition to the war effort.

Unfortunately, by the summer of 1777, the colonial situation had grown bad again. The victory at Trenton seemed a distant memory as the British made advance after advance. But then something happened. The British general John Burgoyne

HESSIANS

Hessians were soldiers from the German state of Hesse hired to fight for the British.

commanded more than 6,000 troops that had come down from Canada and were now gathered near Albany. But these troops were not trained for wilderness fighting. They were prepared to fight in organized formations on open fields. The severely outnumbered Americans had no wish to fight that way—and avoided it whenever possible. Often they staged surprise attacks or fired in skirmishes from behind rocks and trees.

Eventually, Burgoyne had tried to stage a retreat, but by then his supplies were running low. A few bloody skirmishes had shown how ill-suited his men were, even with superior numbers, to fighting in such conditions. On October 17, after several negotiations, Burgoyne surrendered his men and supplies to the Continental forces under the command of General Horatio Gates.

This victory became a turning point for two related reasons: The British realized that that they

In 1777, British commander John Burgoyne surrendered to General Horatio Gates at Saratoga, New York.

could possibly lose this war—
and the French realized that the
Americans could possibly win it.

Naturally, both sides wanted
to talk to Franklin about
the situation. Soon, British
representatives visited Franklin,
Deane, and Lee in Paris. Could
they possibly come to a new
agreement? The Americans
were now poised to take
advantage of their stronger
position. They explained to
the British that any end to the
fighting would have to include

American commissioner Silas
Deane was not as optimistic as
Franklin about America's prospects
for independence.

an acceptance of American independence. The British were
unmoved. They were willing to make many concessions, but
complete independence was not among them.

As for the French, they now saw an opportunity to deal the
British enemy a severe blow. If the Americans could win the
war, the British would lose much of their influence in North
America. This was a worthy goal. So the French stepped up
their support, sending military items such as brass cannons,
muskets, and musket balls, in addition to more everyday
necessities like shoes and tents. The value of this support was
immense, and it came at some cost to the French, whose own
economy was hardly strong.

Most importantly, though, the French sent a fleet of ships. Up to this point, the British fleet had enjoyed almost free rein to move up and down the American coastline. The presence of French ships would make their future movements much more difficult.

Once France and the Americans officially signed a treaty of cooperation, Franklin started making more public appearances. Alarmed at the growing American support in France, the British stepped up their offers to end the conflict. All of the unpopular acts that had been instituted during the past 10 years were revoked. And a degree of independent home rule was proposed. Five years earlier, these conditions would have been happily accepted. Now they were flatly rejected. The Americans were no longer interested in some degree of independence. They wanted it all.

This 1847 painting shows Franklin trying to convince King Louis XVI to support the American cause.

There were still many American defeats to come, but the overall momentum had shifted to their side. In the summer of 1781, Lord Cornwallis, commander of all the British forces, found his army fighting along the coast of southern Virginia. Eventually, it was bottled up on a peninsula in Yorktown. His only chance of escape was by sea, and a fleet of French ships was blocking the way. Cornwallis was trapped. He had no access to fresh supplies, and none would be forthcoming. Finally, on October 19, 1781, he and his 7,000 men surrendered.

The Treaty of Paris, shown here signed by the three American representatives, brought a formal end to the revolution.

The end of the fighting did not mean Franklin could go home, however. He was named, along with fellow members of Congress John Jay and John Adams, to a commission designated to negotiate the peace treaty. The three men brought three different views to the conference table, and they did not always get along. Still, by November 1782, they and their British counterparts had reached a preliminary agreement. On September 3, 1783, the Treaty of Paris was signed and the war was officially over.

chapter **11**

Home at Last

As pleased as Franklin was to have the peace treaties signed and ratified, he knew that not all dangers had passed. Great Britain might have lost the war, but it had not disappeared from the earth. The power of the British Empire was not to be taken lightly. Canada remained British, and it shared a long unguarded border with the northern colonies. Meanwhile the southern colonies were an easy target for the British navy, still the greatest fleet in the world. And even a signed peace treaty was ultimately just a piece of paper.

The British would be on the lookout. If an opportunity presented itself to regain some or all of the colonies, Britain was sure to strike.

Such a situation was not impossible to imagine. Although the colonies had

Joseph Siffred Duplessis'
1778 portrait of Franklin is
perhaps the most well-known
by Americans today.

united to fight the war, it was unclear whether they would stay united in peace. And if they splintered into different groups, they might become weak enough for Great Britain to win them over again at a later date.

Still, none of these worries lessened Franklin's pleasure that peace had been restored. "There was never a good war or a bad peace," he wrote to Josiah Quincy in September 1783. He was truly glad the fighting was over.

But while major political issues filled much of Franklin's time, they did not fill it all. Science continued to draw his attention. He was intrigued about the many advances he saw taking place around him and wondered about those still to come. He speculated about cures for fatal diseases, machines that would defy gravity, and improvements in agriculture that would lead to better crop production.

One new device in particular dramatically stimulated Franklin's thoughts about the future. The idea of flight had been a dream of mankind since at least the days of the ancient Greeks. And now that dream was beginning to come true. Franklin was among the thousands of spectators who saw an early hot-air balloon rise above Paris in August 1783.

VUE DE LA TERRASSE DE Mᵣ FRANKLIN A PASSY.

This engraving shows the 1781 flight of the hot-air balloon as it would have been seen from Franklin's home in Passy.

Supposedly, someone in the crowd was not as impressed as Franklin was by this achievement. He questioned aloud what the use might be of such a balloon. To this, Franklin replied, "What use is a new-born baby?" As far as he was concerned, the possibilities would only reveal themselves over time. It would be foolish to assume that the benefits would not be significant simply because no one could yet imagine them. Still, as enthusiastic as he was about the balloon, Franklin did not believe it would become a common means of transportation in his time.

However, he did think that balloons might dampen the enthusiasm for war. How could a country defend itself against an attack of 5,000 two-man balloons? What ruler, he wondered, could manage to defend his country against "ten thousand men descending from the clouds?" Surely, such a force could "do an infinite amount of mischief before a force could be brought together to repel them."

Never tiring of making his own innovations, Franklin perfected the first bifocal glasses at this time. Over the years he had grown tired of switching between two sets of glasses depending on whether he was reading or looking out over a distance. His idea was to attach half a lens for distance to half a lens for reading, with the distance lens at the top. That way, a single pair of glasses could do both jobs at once. Undoubtedly, others had been similarly frustrated by having to switch between glasses, but, unlike Franklin, they had not directed their attention to solving the problem.

Having spent the last nine years in France, Franklin had many friends who wished him to remain there and enjoy his last years in comfortable retirement. Seventy-nine years old and plagued by various ailments, Franklin could hardly have been looking forward to another ocean voyage. At the same time, he could hardly imagine not seeing Philadelphia again—a free Philadelphia where he would be reunited with his daughter, Sally, her family, and many of his old friends.

So in May 1785, Franklin finally headed for home. Crowds gathered along his route to the coast to cheer him on. After a short visit in England, where he caught up with old friends whose company he had

These early English bifocals clearly show the line between the distance lens and the reading lens.

missed during the war, he boarded a ship for Philadelphia.

This painting shows Franklin being welcomed home by his daughter Sally and son-in-law Richard Bache in Philadelphia.

The voyage home was no better than he expected, but he made the best of it. Upon his arrival in September, Franklin was met with greetings from representatives of many organizations that he had helped to create years before. Among them were the University of Pennsylvania, the Union Fire Company, and the American Philosophical Society. They all wished to honor Franklin, and despite his uncertain health, he was happy to make himself available. Franklin had not intended to take on any new public responsibilities, but when he was asked to be president of Pennsylvania's Supreme Council, which governed the former colony, he did not refuse.

While his body was not the reliable instrument it once had been, Franklin's mind was still active. It was difficult now for him to retrieve books from higher shelves, so he devised another invention to deal with the problem. He called it the "long arm." Basically, it was an eight-foot (2.5 m) long piece of wood joined to a mechanism that allowed him to grab a book at one end by squeezing a grip at the other. He also designed a chair with a built-in cooling fan that he could operate by depressing a pedal with his foot.

But such tinkerings were minor distractions from solving the larger issues that still faced the country. During the Revolution, Congress had created a governing document known as the Articles of Confederation and Perpetual Union. It authorized the new United States government to make war and peace, to print a national currency, and to borrow money for national concerns. The Articles of Confederation had two significant weaknesses, though. First, it did not allow for the national government to collect any taxes. And second, each state had an equal vote in any decisions to be made, regardless of the size of its population.

Franklin and others, including George Washington, could see that this system was not serving the country well.

The Articles of Confederation were circulated throughout the colonies, where they were widely debated.

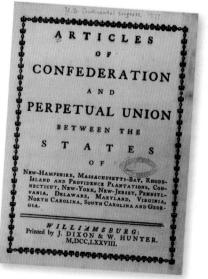

Without the income from taxes, the national government did not have the resources to do much governing. The colonies were operating more like thirteen independent countries than one united one—especially with the threat of war removed for the moment. Changes were needed, and they were needed sooner rather than later if the new nation was to survive.

Although here Franklin is shown standing at the 1787 convention, he actually remained seated most of the time due to his ailments.

In May 1787, a national convention was called in Philadelphia to examine the situation. Fifty-five delegates met to discuss the situation. Their goal was simple on the surface: They needed to create a plan for a strong united country while preserving the rights of individual states. But achieving this goal was complicated. The states had widely varying priorities and many of the delegates distrusted one another. Making them all happy, or happy enough, would not be easy.

James Madison of Virginia (who later became the fourth president of the United States, in 1808) offered what turned out to be the most acceptable plan. It involved creating a central government divided into three branches—executive, legislative, and judicial. The executive branch would be headed by the new office of president. The legislative branch would consist of representatives of Congress, and the judicial branch would be made up of judges, the most powerful of whom would sit on a national Supreme Court. Each of these branches would be a check upon the others. The hope was that these mutual checks would keep the country in a state of healthy equilibrium.

One of the biggest issues was the fear among the little states that the big states would come to dominate them. To keep this from happening, Franklin himself made a helpful suggestion that was quickly picked up by others, including Roger Sherman of Connecticut. He proposed that Congress be split into two houses, one for representatives and the other for senators. The representatives would be elected strictly according to population, so a state with more people would have more representatives. But in the other house, there would be two senators for each state—regardless of how many people happened to live there.

Thanks to Franklin's idea, the modern U.S. Capitol is clearly divided into two wings, one for each house of Congress.

An engraving from around 1800 shows slaves picking cotton on a plantation. Many delegates felt that slavery was immoral.

Although it was not universally loved, this compromise eventually became the law of the land.

After his many years of public service, Franklin recognized that any successful document would require compromise and accommodation on all sides. "When a broad table is to be made," he wrote, "and the edges of the planks do not fit, the artist takes a little from both, and makes a good joint. In like manner here both sides must part with some of their demands, in order that they may join in some accommodating proposition."

One major issue that was not resolved to everyone's satisfaction was that of slavery. Franklin knew that many delegates relied financially on the reality of slaves. Given all the other issues being faced, adding this one to the mix would probably deadlock the convention. The risk was too great. So the issue of slavery, and whether or not it should be allowed to continue, was put aside. It was left for each state to decide for itself.

Franklin knew better than to think the Constitution was perfect, but that didn't trouble him. He didn't know whether it was possible to create a perfect document, "for when you assemble a number of men to have the advantage of their wisdom, you inevitably assemble with those men all the prejudices, their passions, their errors of opinion, the local interests and the selfish views . . . It therefore astonishes me . . . to find this system approaching so near to perfect as it does . . ."

These words were published in many newspapers. The calm confidence they projected influenced a great many people. If Benjamin Franklin, with all his many years of experience, thought that the Constitution would work, why then they thought so, too.

Franklin also knew that other countries, especially England, were waiting for the former colonies to fall apart. He was determined to make sure that didn't happen.

Ratifying the Constitution was clearly going to bring strength and stability to the United States of America.

This 1940 painting of the signing of the Constitution of the United States includes 39 of the 55 delegates present.

chapter **12**

Final Years and Legacy

By the fall of 1788, Franklin realized that he would not be rebounding from his current decline. "Our new Constitution is now established," he wrote in a letter, "and has an appearance that promises permanency; but in the world nothing can be said to be certain except death and taxes." Of death, at least, he was especially certain. In fact, he spent much of his last year in bed suffering from kidney stones. Still, he had few regrets about the life he had led, only sadness that there was so much in the future that he would never witness.

On April 30, 1789, George Washington became the first president of the United States.

This mural detail shows Franklin finally in a real retirement as he received visitors in his garden.

Six months later Congress proposed the Bill of Rights, the first ten amendments to the Constitution (which were ratified in 1791). Franklin was pleased to see that the system was working—that changes could be made, but that they would have to have considerable support to become enacted. (Constitutional Amendments, for example, required the support of three-fourths of the states.)

Benjamin Franklin died on April 17, 1790. Twenty thousand people came to pay their respects—far and away the biggest funeral Philadelphia had ever seen. They were there to honor a man who had been many things: a printer, an inventor, a businessman, a scientist, a politician, a writer, a rebel, and a diplomat. John Adams had written while in France that "there was scarcely a peasant or a citizen, a valet de chamber, coachman or footman, a lady's chambermaid or a scullion in the kitchen who was not familiar with Franklin's name."

No one else of his time, and few people of any time, could make a similar claim. His lifespan linked the memories of those who had known the Pilgrims of Plymouth to those who would lead the new country of the United States through its first important decades.

"Nothing can be said to be certain except death and taxes."

—Benjamin Franklin, in a letter to Jean-Baptiste Leroy

THE LAST RESTING PLACE OF
BENJAMIN FRANKLIN
1706 — 1790

"VENERATED FOR BENEVOLENCE,
ADMIRED FOR TALENTS, ESTEEMED
FOR PATRIOTISM, BELOVED FOR
PHILANTHROPY."

WASHINGTON

"THE SAGE WHOM TWO WORLDS
CLAIMED AS THEIR OWN"

MIRABEAU

"HE TORE FROM THE SKIES THE
LIGHTNING AND FROM TYRANTS
THE SCEPTRE"

TURGOT

This plaque is part of a fenced border to Franklin's gravesite. It includes tributes from some of his contemporaries.

Just as importantly, Franklin left a distinctly American legacy behind him. A working man's son with little formal education, he had risen to the highest levels of both the scientific and political worlds. He had shown by his own example that intelligence, sacrifice, and dedication were powerful tools in the pursuit of a successful life. And his accomplishments have inspired many in the generations that have followed him.

Yet, while mindful of his many achievements, Franklin did not in the end see the need to boast of them. The only words originally on his tomb were the plain ones he had chosen: "BENJAMIN AND DEBORAH FRANKLIN 1790."

But it is worth remembering the more playful epitaph he had written for himself years before at the age of 22 (and which now appear on a plaque near his grave):

The body of
B. Franklin, Printer
(Like the Cover of an Old Book
Its Contents torn Out

And Stript of its Lettering and Gilding)
Lies Here, Food for Worms.
But the Work shall not be Lost;
For it will (as he Believ'd) Appear once More
In a New and More Elegant Edition
Revised and Corrected
By the Author.

Franklin's achievements were many, and no doubt he took pride in them all. But set above his personal accomplishments was his awareness that he had been part of an extraordinary experiment, the founding of a nation based on principles unparalleled in the history of the world. And he had hopes that those principles, which he believed firmly anchored his new country, would spread elsewhere over time. In one of his last letters to a friend in England, Franklin wrote: "God grant that not only the love of liberty, but a thorough knowledge of the rights of man, may pervade all the nations of the earth, so that a philosopher may set his foot anywhere on its surface, and say, 'This is my country.'"

John J. Boyle's 1899 statue of Benjamin Franklin in Paris shows the American in thoughtful repose.

16ᵉ Arrᵗ
RUE
BENJAMIN
FRANKLIN
(1706 - 1790)
PHYSICIEN ET HOMME D'ÉTAT
AMÉRICAIN

Events in the Life of Benjamin Franklin

1724
Franklin makes first trip to London, planning to buy a printing press. He ends up staying for two years.

1757
Franklin returns to England as the colonial agent for Pennsylvania. He will stay for five years.

1728
Franklin establishes his first printing business with Hugh Meredith. Franklin soon buys out Meredith's share.

1706
Benjamin Franklin is born on January 17 in Boston, Massachusetts.

1741
Franklin invents the Franklin Stove.

1732
Franklin publishes the first edition of *Poor Richard's Almanack*, which will be a success for the next 25 years.

1748
Franklin retires from business with enough money to live comfortably.

1718
Franklin becomes an apprentice to his brother James, a printer.

1723
Franklin leaves Boston after a falling out with James and settles in Philadelphia. He meets his future wife, Deborah Read.

1752
Franklin conducts his electricity experiment with a kite, the latest chapter in a nine-year investigation of electricity.

1762
Franklin returns to
Philadelphia.

1764
Franklin returns to
England for the third
time, beginning an
11-year stay.

1776
Franklin helps draft
the Declaration of
Independence, which
is announced on July
4. In the fall, he goes
to France to plead the
American cause.

1783
Franklin signs the Treaty of Paris,
which officially ends the war with
Great Britain. He invents bifocals
to eliminate the need to carry two
pairs of glasses.

1785
Franklin returns home to
Philadelphia. He accepts
the Presidency of the
Pennsylvania Executive
Council.

1775
As a member of
the Continental
Congress, Franklin
advocates
separation from
England.

1787
Franklin signs the
Constitution of the
United States.

1790
Benjamin Franklin
dies on April 17.

1778
Franklin arranges the
American alliance with
France, a crucial step
toward the eventual
success of the
Revolution.

1771
Franklin begins
to write his
autobiography.

Bibliography

Brands, H.W. *The First American: The Life and Times of Benjamin Franklin*. New York: Doubleday, 2000.

Clark, Ronald W. *Benjamin Franklin: A Biography*. New York: Random House, 1983.

Dray, Philip. *Stealing God's Thunder: Benjamin Franklin's Lightning Rod and the Invention of America*. New York: Random House, 2005.

Fleming, Thomas, ed. *Benjamin Franklin: A Biography in His Own Words*. New York: Harper & Row, 1972.

Franklin, Benjamin. *Franklin: Autobiography and Later Writings*. New York: The Library of America, 1987.

Hawke, David Freeman. *Everyday Life in Early America*. New York: Harper & Row, 1988.

Kaplan, Justin, ed. *Bartlett's Familiar Quotations*. Boston: Little, Brown and Company, 1992.

Isaacson, Walter. *Benjamin Franklin*. New York: Simon and Schuster, 2003.

Meltzer, Milton. *Benjamin Franklin: The New American*. New York: Franklin Watts, 1988.

Paine, Thomas. *Common Sense and Other Political Writings*. Indianapolis: The Bobbs-Merrill Company, 1953.

Smyth, Albert Henry. *The Writings of Benjamin Franklin*. New York: The Macmillan Company, 1907.

Taylor, Alan. *American Colonies*. New York: Viking, 2001.

Thomas, Isaiah. *The History of Printing in America*. Barre, MA: The Imprint Society, 1970.

Works Cited

p. 9: "the Reflection gave me more Chagrin . . ." *Benjamin Franklin: A Biography in His Own Words*, page 17

p. 18: "I bought it, read it over and over . . ." *Franklin: Autobiography, Poor Richard and Later Writings*, page 579

p. 19: "Verse-makers were generally beggars . . ." *Franklin: Autobiography, Poor Richard and Later Writings*, page 578

p. 20: "middle-aged widow . . ." "a hearty Lover of the Clergy . . ." *Benjamin Franklin: A Biography in His Own Words*, page 24

p. 23: "a Boy of but 17 . . ." *Franklin: Autobiography, Poor Richard and Later Writings*, page 586

p. 26: "These two printers . . ." *Franklin: Autobiography, Poor Richard and Later Writings*, page 591

p. 27: "star'd like a Pig poison'd" *Franklin: Autobiography, Poor Richard and Later Writings*, page 593

p. 29: "I had great respect . . ." *Franklin: Autobiography and Later Writings*, page 600

p. 30: "told me there was not the least Probability . . ." *Franklin: Autobiography, Poor Richard and Later Writings*, page 604

p. 33: "1. It is necessary for me to be extremely frugal . . ." *Benjamin Franklin: A Biography in His Own Words*, pages 50–51

p. 36: "a paltry thing" *Benjamin Franklin: Franklin: Autobiography, Poor Richard and Later Writings*, page 623

p. 38: "assisted me cheerfully . . ." *Benjamin Franklin: A Biography in His Own Words*, page 59

p. 40: "Courteous Reader . . ." *Benjamin Franklin: Franklin: Autobiography, Poor Richard and Later Writings*, page 445

p. 42: "If you would not be forgotten . . ." *Franklin: Autobiography, Poor Richard and Later Writings*, page 468

p. 45: "In order to secure my Credit . . ." *Franklin: Autobiography, Poor Richard and Later Writings*, page 629

p. 45: "Finding that I can live in this manner . . ." *The History of Printing in America*, page 370

p. 46: "Temperance: Eat not to dullness ..." *Franklin: Autobiography, Poor Richard and Later Writings*, pages 644–645

p. 48: "Knowledge is power." *Bartlett's Familiar Quotations*, p. 158

p. 51: "We enjoy great advantages ..." *Franklin: Autobiography, Poor Richard and Later Writings*, pages 677–678

p.54: "was not created by friction ... " *Benjamin Franklin: A Biography in His Own Words*, page 87

p. 60: "I leave them to take their chance ..." *Benjamin Franklin: The New American*, page 131

p. 64: "Almost every war between the Indians and whites ..." *Benjamin Franklin: The New American*, page 147

p. 70: "to live in a fashion and expense ..." *The Writings of Benjamin Franklin*, page 213

p. 73: "happy and truly glorious" *The Writings of Benjamin Franklin*, page 209

p. 78: "able to shake off any shackle ..." *Benjamin Franklin: The New American*, page 198

p. 89: "Mr. Strahan: You are a member of Parliament ..." *Franklin: Autobiography and Later Writings*, page 165

p. 92: "These are the times ..." *Common Sense and Other Political Writings*, page 55

p. 92: "Those who expect to reap ..." *Bartlett's Familiar Quotations*, page 341

p. 94: "We hold these truths to be self-evident ..." *Benjamin Franklin: An American Life*, page 312

p. 95: "We must all hang together ..." *Benjamin Franklin: An American Life*, page 313

p. 100: "The wit of conversation ..." *Benjamin Franklin: The New American*, page 238

p. 103: "Justice is as strictly due ..." *Benjamin Franklin: The New American*, page 250

p. 103: "to be concerned in no affairs ..." *Benjamin Franklin: The New American*, page 244

p. 109: "There was never a good war ..." *Bartlett's Familiar Quotations*, page 310

p. 110: "What use is a new-born baby?" *Benjamin Franklin: An American Life*, page 421

p. 110: "ten thousand men descending from the clouds ... do an infinite amount of mischief ..." *Benjamin Franklin: A Biography*, page 389

p. 116: "When a broad table is to be made ..." *Benjamin Franklin: The New American*, page 264

p. 116: " ... for when you assemble a number of men ..." *Franklin: Autobiography, Poor Richard and Later Writings*, page 400

p. 118: "Our new Constitution is now established ..." *Benjamin Franklin: A Biography in His Own Words*, page 403

p. 119: "there was scarcely a peasant ..." *Benjamin Franklin: An American Life*, page 327

p. 121: "The body of B. Franklin ..." *Benjamin Franklin: A Biography in His Own Words*, page 129

p. 121: "God grant that not only the love of liberty ..." *Benjamin Franklin: A Biography*, pages 412–413

For Further Study

The *Autobiography of Benjamin Franklin* provides an intimate look at some of the events, thoughts, and motivations that characterized Franklin's life.

Visit Philadelphia, the site of Independence Hall and the Liberty Bell, among other colonial hallmarks. Although none of Franklin's homes have survived, you can still follow in his footsteps by walking down some of Philadelphia's oldest streets, starting with Market Street, where he first arrived in 1723.

Visit the Old Granary Burial Ground in the middle of Boston, Massachusetts, where Josiah Franklin is buried under a large monument—placed there by his son Benjamin.

The Library of Congress maintains an extensive collection of Franklin's works and papers. You can find it at www.loc.gov/exhibits/treasures/franklin-home.html

Index

Acknowledgments

My thanks to Dan Terris, who wears several hats at Brandeis University, for his thoughtful comments on the manuscript, and to my editor John Searcy for helping to shepherd me through the DK process.

Picture Credits

The photographs in this book are used with permission and through the courtesy of:

The Image Works: pp.1, 111 SSPL

Alamy Images: pp.2–3, 79 Print Collector; pp.7, 25, 64, 80, 86, 99, 104, 122TL North Wind Picture Archive; p.14 imagebroker; p.17 Lebrecht Music and Arts Photo Library; p.30 Dagleish Images; pp.48, 58, 62, 67, 68, 96, 101, 110, 122BR, 124–125, 126–127 Visual Arts Library (London); p.50 Steve Hamblin; p.70 David Pearson; p.72 The National Trust Photolibrary; p.77 Mary Evans Picture Library; p.89 Tetra Images; p.108 Stockdisc Classic (frame); p.115 JTB Photo Communications, Inc.; p.120 m-images

Bridgeman Art Library: pp.5, 94, 123TL Private Collection; p.34 New York Historical Society; p.97 American Antiquarian Society

Boston Public Library: p.6

Yale University Library: p.8

American Philosophical Society: pp.9, 29, 55, 61, 106

Corbis: pp.10, 21, 23 Bettman; p.12 Owen Franken; p.90 Francis G. Mayer; pp.107, 123TR Corbis

Jupiter Images: p.11

Benjamin Franklin Institute of Technology/Charles Mills Murals: pp.15, 46, 95, 118 (Bakman Zonoozi), 122BL

Getty Images: pp.16, 19, 32, 36, 71, 75, 116; pp.28, 41, 42, 73; 76, 102 Time and Life Pictures; pp.59, 60 Roger Viollet

The Historic Society of Pennsylvania: pp.18, 27T

Massachusetts Historical Society: p.20

Art Resource: pp.22, 39, 43 The New York Public Library; p.54 Erich Lessing; pp.66, 108 National Portrait Gallery/Smithsonian Institution; p.74 The Philadelphia Museum of Art; p.78 Art Resource; p.93 HIP-British Museum; pp.121, 123BR Timothy McCarthy

Library of Congress: pp.24, 40, 49, 57, 65, 82, 83, 85, 87, 88, 91, 92, 98, 105, 113, 114, 122BC

New York Public Library: pp.27B, 38

Beinecke Rare Book and Manuscript Library: pp.33, 47, 53

The Library Company of Philadelphia: pp.37, 44, 45

North Wind Picture Archive: pp.52, 122TR

Harvard University Art Museums/Fogg Art Museum/Bequest of Dr. John Collins Warren, President and Fellow of Harvard College: p.56 Katya Kallsen (photographer)

Frick Art Library: p.69

SuperStock: p.81 Stock Montage; pp.84, 100, 112, 123BL SuperStock

Architect of the Capitol: pp.117, 123BTR

BORDER PHOTOS from left to right:
Alamy Images (Visual Arts Library, London); Alamy Images (North Wind Picture Archive); Alamy Images (Stephen Saks Photography); American Philosophical Society; Architect of the Capitol; Getty Images; Library of Congress; Benjamin Franklin Institute of Technology (Charles Mills Murals); Alamy Images (The Print Collector); Benjamin Franklin Institute of Technology (Charles Mills Murals); SuperStock (Stock Montage); American Philosophical Society; Library of Congress; Getty Images; Superstock; Alamy Images (Visual Arts Library, London) Benjamin Franklin Institute of Technology (Charles Mills Murals/Bakman Zonoozi)

About the Author

Stephen Krensky is the author of more than 100 fiction and nonfiction books for children including historical works on George Washington, the Wright Brothers, American comic books, and the invention of the printing press. He lives in Lexington, Massachusetts, with his wife Joan and their family.

Other DK Biographies you'll enjoy:

Joan of Arc
Kay Kudlinski
ISBN 978-0-7566-3526-8 paperback
ISBN 978-0-7566-3527-5 hardcover

Charles Darwin
David C. King
ISBN 978-0-7566-2554-2 paperback
ISBN 978-0-7566-2555-9 hardcover

Princess Diana
Joanne Mattern
ISBN 978-0-7566-1614-4 paperþack
ISBN 978-0-7566-1613-7 hardcover

Amelia Earhart
Tanya Lee Stone
ISBN 978-0-7566-2552-8 paperback
ISBN 978-0-7566-2553-5 hardcover

Albert Einstein
Frieda Wishinsky
ISBN 978-0-7566-1247-4 paperback
ISBN 978-0-7566-1248-1 hardcover

Gandhi
Amy Pastan
ISBN 978-0-7566-2111-7 paperback
ISBN 978-0-7566-2112-4 hardcover

Harry Houdini
Vicki Cobb
ISBN 978-0-7566-1245-0 paperback
ISBN 978-0-7566-1246-7 hardcover

Helen Keller
Leslie Garrett
ISBN 978-0-7566-0339-7 paperback
ISBN 978-0-7566-0488-2 hardcover

John F. Kennedy
Howard S. Kaplan
ISBN 978-0-7566-0340-3 paperback
ISBN 978-0-7566-0489-9 hardcover

Martin Luther King, Jr.
Amy Pastan
ISBN 978-0-7566-0342-7 paperback
ISBN 978-0-7566-0491-2 hardcover

Abraham Lincoln
Tanya Lee Stone
ISBN 978-0-7566-0834-7 paperback
ISBN 978-0-7566-0833-0 hardcover

Nelson Mandela
Lenny Hort & Laaren Brown
ISBN 978-0-7566-2109-4 paperback
ISBN 978-0-7566-2110-0 hardcover

Annie Oakley
Chuck Wills
ISBN 978-0-7566-2997-7 paperback
ISBN 978-0-7566-2986-1 hardcover

Pelé
Jim Buckley
ISBN 978-0-7566-2987-8 paperback
ISBN 978-0-7566-2996-0 hardcover

Eleanor Roosevelt
Kem Knapp Sawyer
ISBN 978-0-7566-1496-6 paperback
ISBN 978-0-7566-1495-9 hardcover

George Washington
Lenny Hort
ISBN 978-0-7566-0835-4 paperback
ISBN 978-0-7566-0832-3 hardcover

Look what the critics are saying about DK Biography!

"…highly readable, worthwhile overviews for young people…" —*Booklist*

"This new series from the inimitable DK Publishing brings together the usual brilliant photography with a historian's approach to biography subjects." —*Ingram Library Services*